Books of Passage

also edited by David Perkins

Raleigh:
A Living History of North Carolina's Capital

Pete & Shirley:
The Great Tar Heel Novel

Books of Passage

27 North Carolina Writers on the Books that Changed Their Lives

Edited by David Perkins

Illustrated by David Terry

Down Home Press, Asheboro, North Carolina

First Printing— January 1997
1 2 3 4 5 6 7 8 9

ISBN 1-878086-53-7

Library of Congress Catalog Card Number
96-085572

Printed in the United States of America

Cover art by David Terry
Book design by Beth Glover

Down Home Press
P.O. Box 4126
Asheboro, N.C. 27204

Dedication

For Barbara, Joan, John and Tracy —
in love and gratitude

'Camerado, this is no book,
who touches this, touches a man,
(Is it night? Are we here alone?)
It is I you hold, and who holds you,
I spring from the pages into your arms...'

— Walt Whitman

Table of Contents

Books of Passage

Introduction

by David Perkins

As W.H. Auden once said, we don't read books, they read us.

A good book takes us off the shelf, dusts us off, and turns our pages until it finds something with a capacity for feeling, a sense of wonder or beauty that we hadn't suspected was in us.

A philosopher or a scientist might have a problem with this assertion, but we know it's true. Perhaps we forget it. An adolescent knows with certainty that he's on an equal footing with Emerson or Tolstoy. How thrilling to find writers who know us to the core, better even than we know ourselves. (And certainly better than our parents!)

It's usually in adolecsence or early adulthood that one encounters the book that stirs us in this way. It can't be a book that someone else has chosen for us. We have to choose *it* — out of curiosity, desire, unconscious need, whatever is seeking to grow in us, and not because an authority has presented it as "worthy" or "uplifting." The choice is what makes it a rite of passage.

No wonder, then, that we remember exactly where and how we found our significant book — how it smelled and felt — and where we spent our private moments with it. Like our first love.

These essays appeared, one a month, over three and a half years in *The News & Observer's* book review pages. As the series unfolded, I was surprised by two things. First, I had thought there would be some overlapping choices. Except for two bids for *Madame Bovary* — that's surprising, too — every one chose a different book. The significant book is as singular as our other important choices.

I had also expected some of our writers to choose a fantasy, mystery or adventure book — the common stuff of teen reading. *Hurlbut's Story of the Bible* might be put in this category, and so too might *Bulfinch's Mythology*. But, as Doris Betts writes in her account, it was the reality of the Hurlbut's Old Testament stories — especially the strong women and the rough justices they sometimes encountered — that impressed her. And Janet Lembke was interested in the Greek gods' *grands amours*. Generally, it seems, the significant books are intensely grown-up.

For Robert Morgan, the pictures and passions of Tolstoy's Moscow and St. Petersburg suggested a world beyond his Blue Ridge town that, nevertheless, belonged to him. For Reynolds Price, Emma Bovary's deluded romance transported him to a place more heated than Raleigh's Five Points — Flaubert's Paris — but not than the young Price's mind and heart.

Like those two writers, Clyde Edgerton was in high school when he encounted his significant book: Emerson's *Essays*, which counseled self-reliance and independent thinking — unlike what he'd heard in Sunday school.

Jerry Bledsoe was 21 when he read Reynolds Price's first novel and met eastern North Carolinians whose story seemed to explain something of his own story, and his own desires.

When they came upon their book of passage, Fred Hobson and John Shelton Reed were entering graduate school in the early '60s and looking for something to help them understand the changing South and their mission in it. They found — or were found by — two quite different books: W.J. Cash's *Mind of the South* and the Agrarians' *I'll Take My Stand.* Hal Crowther shows how a significant book such as *Cry, the Beloved Country* can gather meaning as it is reread over a lifetime.

Generally, our writers don't talk about finding inspiration or a vocation in their significant book. Nevertheless, for a few, it helped them solve a central problem of their identity as writers. Lee Smith had told stories from her childhood on — it was not a trait her relatives applauded — but she didn't know how to write about what she knew best — the life and folk of Grundy, Virginia — until she came upon the fiction of Appalachian writer James Still. Wordsworth and William Carlos Williams helped James Applewhite find the wellspring of his own poetry in common epiphanies and the language of plain speaking people.

In a few cases, a book changed our writer's life in middle age. Robert Pirsig's *Zen and the Art of Motorcycle Maintenace* challenged Jane Tompkins, stuck in career doldrums, to test the riskier side of her nature. Fred Chappell was a young professor when Julia Child altered his life and his waistline.

Taken together, these essays offer an intimate look into the early lives of some of North Carolina's best writers. They also can be read as an intimate history of the mid-century South, and the place of books and reading in a region where the word has always had special significance. But, for me, again and again, they brought home one particular conclusion: The great books give us passage to ourselves.

James Applewhite

---

on

William Wordsworth and

William Carlos Williams

james applewhite
DAVID TERRY 8/96

For years during my young manhood, I'd been haunted by a set of persistent images, some of them dreams and some of them dreamlike memories.

In one of these, I was a boy looking through the fly-specked porch screen as I lay on an outside couch, sick with rheumatic fever. I watched my father in his Esso coveralls as he pushed the old reel mower across the grass in the August twilight. I felt how this hard-handed man who didn't know how to relate to his ill son, nevertheless, in his stiff, erect pushing of the mower, held me back from the threat of my illness.

This scene had stuck with me ever since. But it wasn't until I was at Duke University in the mid-'60s, working on my Ph.D., that I discovered how to work it into a poem. Here's how it came out. I still kind of like it.

Lawn and Light

His mower whirred cut grass like dust
Through daylight gray as if seen through windowscreen,
spun
Raw cut scent of wiregrass into the dusk.
His short muscular figure strained erect
While I was prostrate on the sideporch couch with
fever,
But I knew from intensely seeing
The light raining gray over his stiff effort
Bringing the night with lawnmower sleepier than
crickets
That he was becoming a part of me forever.
I knew even then the sadness of a memory
To be, even as the shape of his strength

And turn of his mower, sweet
Like the strained music of a summer fan,
Held me from dying.

At last, this read like something of my own. Under the influence of two poets, William Wordsworth and William Carlos Williams, I had found my voice. It reflected my experience, my people — and, a little at least, the way they talked quietly on sidewalks and porches.

It had taken me a long time to find these masters. As an undergraduate, my admiration had been for those elegant, internationalized poets of the earlier 20th century, whose learned visions of historic fragmentation had no relation to my own experience. What could W.B. Yeats' impersonal gyres symbolizing the cycles of history, or T.S. Eliot's *The Waste Land*, have to do with the world I remembered, the world Down East? Eliot had represented the mind's "heap of broken images" (*The Waste Land*), but I refused to believe that no hope of coherence existed.

Still, I'd have to put things together for myself, and to interpret, or read, my own interior images, I needed the experience-based poems of Wordsworth and Williams. Their clues to a meaningfulness in ordinary things helped me understand my own psyche.

I'd met Wordsworth at UNC-Greensboro (then Women's College), as I prepared to teach a literature class. He was one of my mentor Randall Jarrell's favorites, and Jarrell talked enough about him to heighten my interest. What appealed to me originally were Wordsworth's "spots of time" — a phrase he uses in *The Prelude* to indicate certain indelible scenes implanted by nature in his childhood. These are moments that persist in the mind, even below the level of consciousness, to return later when the understanding is ready for them.

Two of these came to my mind when I was writing *Lawn and Light*. In the first, Wordsworth is waiting to be taken home from school, for a vacation during which his father will die. He looks anxiously up the road into the "wind and sleety rain," his eyes "intensely straining." In the other, he has lost track of the servant who was guiding him across a desolate moor. After passing the spot where a murderer once had been hanged, he sees a "visionary dreariness" extending over the landscape, to envelop a solitary woman climbing under a burden toward a hill-top beacon, her "garments vexed and tossed/By the strong wind." He would need, he says, "Colours and words that are unknown to man" to explain the existential mixture of despair and courage that this "ordinary sight" depicts.

When I read these lines, I immediately identified with the loss of father and the threat of extinction — and with the purpose and endurance of the woman's journey.

For I had my *own* spots of time, rooted in my early life in a farming village in eastern North Carolina. Things both comforting and frightening, both admirable and depressing, had continued to exist in imagination, like a series of pictures with the captions erased.

There was the lumbermill fire, with flames licking near the bomblike gasoline storage tanks.

There was my grandfather pushing his handplow in his backyard garden; there was the crowd in our Methodist Church on a revival evening, and the unbroken Edenic skin of our swimming pond in its circle of willows — with the great snake that had one day twisted through the gatelike branches.

And there was the general store my grandfather had lost in the Depression: cavernous spaces with horsecollars, peanuts, carriage bolts, shotguns, tobacco twine, rubber boots and basketed sweet potatoes, my grandfather's name still hovering across them in the ghostly gold letters of the plate glass window.

If I was ever to become a poet, I needed to learn to read the inscriptions that contained the clues to my own history, illegible as they seemed to be. Eventually I would read in the expressions of black faces and white, the legacy of a ruined tobacco culture that one time had held slaves — inscriptions bleaker than I'd imagined, but authentic, at last, relevant to me.

It was Wordsworth who helped me see these thought-pictures as material for poetry. He gave me the vision — an ability to see wholeness, and life, to find even in depression and remembered pain the sources of strength and a poetry of endurance.

But I still didn't have everything I needed. The language that for Wordsworth was fresh and natural sometimes sounded stilted and distant to my American ears. I couldn't quite use phrases like his, good as they were. That "vexed and tossed" was wonderful, but a little stiff, a little Miltonic.

This is where William Carlos Williams came to my aid. At Duke, preparing for my Ph.D. orals, I was auditing a course taught by Bernard Duffey, a wise, kindly, deeply insightful teacher. Duffey made me see how Williams' vivid simplicities, which at first had seemed without charm, were very close to Wordsworth's.

Both poets valued the lives and language of those who lived in humble, vivid circumstances. They shared what I thought of as a Beatitudes vision. The "least of these" upon whom the imagination's attention fell were worthy of poetry. It was not necessary that events be international or apocalyptic — not "hooded hordes swarming/ Over endless plains.../ Ringed by the flat horizon only" (*The Waste Land*), but particular figures, like Williams' "big young bareheaded woman in an apron" looking into her shoe to find the nail "that has been hurting her" (*Proletarian Portrait*). And the language that embodied Williams' women and men held a rugged love and realism that conveyed their import and dignity.

I sensed in Williams' poetry, as in Wordsworth's, the record of some indestructible vitality. "By the road to the contagious hospital" the good doctor saw the "forked, upstanding, twiggy stuff of bushes and small trees" re-enter life (*Spring and All*), in phrases that suggest the births of infants: "naked, cold, uncertain of all save that they enter." Though the meanings were "uncertain," birth and continuity exerted their hopeful pressure.

Williams and Wordsworth gave me what I'd wanted: a poetry that could praise and help perpetuate the soil and water and growth, the lovingness and heartaches of humans in their landscape. They showed me how to value in language the crucial goods of life, which power and pride and wealth and contention are so configured as to trample on or ignore. That Williams could write a poem about a subject no more famous or heralded than a "Young Sycamore" inspired me.

One evening during the year in Durham when I was first reading Williams, my wife and I were preparing for bed in our house on somewhat-pastoral Pickett Road. It had been a good day. Our three young children had gone off to sleep, for once peacefully. My wife, the girl I'd loved in childhood and had married as an undergraduate, said sleepily that she thought she heard it raining.

I went out into the night to see whether I might have left the windows down in our car. It was early fall. In that moment, the young maple in a yard across the street, gathering the rain-sound inside its leaves, communicated with me like another living being — which it was. I heard its listening. Helped by Wordsworth's sense of nature, and by Williams' poems to growing things, I came inside and wrote *Tree in the Rain* — the first poem of mine to join the two crucial literary influences that would enable my later books. Here it is, pretty much as I jotted it down then.

Tree in the Rain

I came out into the wet night
Wondering if windows of my car were down.
Keen drops needed into the slick grass.
The town was deep in a rustle of rain
Fresh-smelling as flapping wash.
I settled into a chair, willing to wait,

Thought of the earthworms stirring —

Still, in spite of my drowse
The young tree shaped like a cloud
Across the street seemed poised, aware.
I sensed the inside of it rain-rubbery,
Clammy like a wet raincoat,
With scratching branches and with leaf-edges
That would tickle like bugs;

And yet it dreamed itself
Listening like the ears of earthworms
Under their lids of mud.
A sensation trickled into me of it
Risen like an earth-pulse into the showering
Sky, like a single cupped palm
Catching drink, or cupped, hearing.

I felt the cold sound naked on my skin.

I notice that I made the suburban neighborhood a "town," and associated the rain's smell with that of wash on a clothesline — a detail from Down East, not Durham. But poetry puts things together.

When I returned to Greensboro, I took with me a partially finished dissertation on Wordsworth's *Prelude*, and a few poems that seemed my own. It felt a bit curious that I'd found a voice for myself in the coming together of two writers so separated by distance and time. But after all, I thought, doesn't poetry leap over those differences and distinctions that seem so immutable to our literal-mindedness?

As with love, in poetry we may find ourselves by finding someone else.

James Applewhite is a native of Wilson County and currently is Professor of English at Duke University. His six books of poetry include Statues of the Grass *and* Lessons in Soaring. *He was awarded the 1992 Jean Stein Award in Poetry from the American Academy and Institute of Arts and Letters.*

Daphne Athas

---

on

Leo Tolstoy's

Confessions

Daphne Athas
DAVID TERRY 96

Books became a life and death issue when I had my first boyfriend, Wayne.

We met in high school when we were both about 15. I was from the North, and our family had lost our money in the Depression, so we lived in a shack near the black section of Chapel Hill. It was full of books, my mother's Bronte and Dickens, my father's Dewey, Pierce, Greek lexicons, and Homer.

My father was a Greek immigrant, opinionated, egalitarian and colorful. He praised America to the skies because he had come here and instead of going to work in a restaurant like most Greeks he had gone to college and law school. He liked Wayne a lot. He also liked the fact that Wayne came from millworkers.

Most of my friends were scared by Daddy's intellectual arrogance, but not Wayne. He was fascinated. He hadn't grown up with books in the house, but because of the Carrboro school system and his brains he'd read everything. At supper Daddy would challenge him with philosophical questions about virtue or knowledge. Wayne jumped into these Socratic dialogues with both feet, and over time got adept at sidestepping Daddy's arguments. This made my father laugh.

Wayne confided to me that when he was 10 he had been "saved" in a revival tent. I couldn't believe it. Our family had gone to Congregational Sunday school until Mother found out we were coloring Christ with crayons. She said Jesus was a good man who led the world in doing unto others what you would have them do unto you, and we should follow his example. Daddy sneered at the superstitious side of religion.

Yet religion became a keystone of my friendship with Wayne. He and I would walk along Carrboro's dirt streets and talk. I always took the anti-religious side, exclaiming how amazed I was that people could believe so much sanctimonious baloney. Wayne loved my outrageousness, but it put him in a quandary. He had lost his Baptist "faith," he said, and it was since he'd met me. It wasn't my fault, I argued. He admitted books might be responsible, too. But that only made him read more. I watched him seize on every book like a magpie, ravenous for the truth of meaning or religion, plugging into every new thing without discrimination.

I longed for meaning too, but since I hadn't had that kind of faith, I was less aggressive. Wayne talked about Leibnitz, Kant and Horace Williams, who owned the mill house he lived in. Since age 12 Wayne had taken the four dollars rent money to the philosopher every month, gazing at his books through the screen door. He wrote me a letter once about Horace Williams' autobiography: "He reached almost the same conclusion that I did. An atheist is a person who has lived without meeting a crisis which has given him a need for the personal power from some source inside him." Wayne joined the Literary Guild of America to get the bonus volumes of the Bible, the Koran, the Talmud and other religious literature.

Our bookishness gave us a common bond against high school conformity, and we clung together, alienated and arrogant. I blamed my unpopularity on homemade clothes and poverty and embraced ugliness. Wayne blamed Carrboro and parents who hadn't gone past eighth grade. Our senior year the English teacher warned us that *War and Peace* was inappropriate to do book reports on, but we ignored him and did it anyway.

When we entered college, we became closer and even more defensive. In the full rush of adolescence we experimented with beer and sex in the Episcopal cloister, writing our reactions down, using key words such as "compensation" from Freud and "futility" from the Russian novels. We never asked our parents about orgasm, desire or violence. Instead we went to the rare book room and read Havelock Ellis and Kraft-Ebing. One night, dazed on the library steps under the moon, we vowed to always search for the answer to life.

Later, alone in the stacks I was overcome by futility. It was during a football game. I had to write a term paper. Roman mobs were emitting roars in Kenan Stadium, but what I wanted was Truth. Remembering how Tolstoy had Pierre ask the meaning of life in *War and Peace*, I poked through the card catalog for clues.

There was Tolstoy's *Confessions*. I got goose bumps. I didn't know he had written a confession. In the stacks I found the musty volume, and the first line was "I was baptized and brought up in the Orthodox Christian faith.... But when I left the second course of the university at the age of 18, I no longer believed in any of the things I had been taught." Tolstoy wrote this when he was past 50, famous and happily married with children.

"What will come of my whole life?" he asked himself. "Is there anything in my life that the inevitable death awaiting me will not destroy?"

Mankind is like a traveler, he said, quoting an Eastern parable. The traveler is being chased by a monster and has fallen down a dry well where he catches himself on a twig. At the bottom is a roaring dragon, death. Above is the monster, death. As he holds on, two mice approach and gnaw the twig. He sees upon the leaf some drops of honey, the pleasures of temporal life, which he reaches out and licks with his tongue.

In spite of the bleakness of this tale, I was seized with joy. Another shout went up in the stadium. The fact that Tolstoy could be dead and say this to me through half a century's divide was awesome. Not the Truth of life. Not an answer. But an analogy.

Twenty years later in my novel, *Entering Ephesus*,

I wrote about the naive vow on the library steps. Our lives were so interwoven that Wayne and I were parts of each others' vocabularies. We could not separate even when our lives separated. While he was in the Army and I in New York, through his stint in China and mine in Europe, past his marriage and family and my career, the friendship persisted because no one else shared such a twinship of literature and adolescent angst. It is documented in its lonely wonder and we still honor it. "Why is it," I wrote him only the other day, "that analogy can be as thrilling as an answer?"

Daphne Athas, born in Cambridge, Massachusetts, moved to Chapel Hill early in life. She has written fiction, nonfiction, poems, plays and essays.

Doris Betts

on

Hurlbut's Story of the Bible for Young and Old

DAVID TERRY 8/96
DORIS BETTS

In The Bookshop in Chapel Hill recently, I was scanning the spines of used books in search of something else when a familiar title leaped out like the full name of a half-forgotten friend suddenly recognized through layers of age and wear. The color was wrong, the binding ugly. In my older hand, the book weighed less than I remembered.

But I could look straight through its pages and find again its long-ago counterpart spread wide on the linoleum and hear myself calling, "Here's another word I don't know!"

"Spell it," my father would mumble, unwilling to leave his radio.

I did — four syllables, maybe five, capitalized — spelled it again until he let out a short, sharp word and after a cross look at my mother, came to see what geographical piece of Canaan my thumbnail underlined.

Under his teaching, using the Sunday comic strips as his text, I had learned to read between ages four and five. The simple language matched the cartoon pictures and suited the characters.

But my churchgoing mother may have mistrusted simplicity. She — a cradle Associate Reformed Presbyterian — knew that he (at that time, a fallen-away Methodist) took obvious enjoyment in reading pulp Westerns. She may have doubted that the Katzenjammer Kids, the quarrelsome Maggie and Jiggs, or Flash Gordon with his half-dressed female friends, provided suitable moral examples. Or perhaps she thought it was a quick downhill trip from the funny papers to the blood-and-thunder magazines my father kept stacked behind the sofa.

So when a door-to-door salesman came by, selling leather-bound copies of *Hurlbut's Story of the Bible for*

Young and Old, she put five hard-earned dollars down and paid a dollar per week until the $11 had bought my fifth birthday present, 757 pages of 168 stories, "running," it said on the frontispiece, "from Genesis to Revelation."

The Rev. Jesse Lyman Hurlbut, D.D., first copyrighted the book in 1904. It was profusely illustrated with what I took to be literal depictions like the photos that appeared in the *Statesville Record*. These two in leafy tunics were the real Adam and Eve; Ishmael actually went naked into the desert while Hagar carried their meager rations in this very basket on her head; Nebuchadnezzar's fiery furnace deserved its full page as colorful as Blondie and Dagwood.

Unlike the balloons above comic characters, these flat statements underneath each picture confirmed my certainty that the pictures were factual. "Jonah Thrown Overboard by the Sailors," one caption said. "Judas Kisses Jesus in the Garden." In the summary listing of illustrations, no mention was made of paintings or artists.

I didn't quite understand, though, why Samson had taken all his clothes off before wrestling a lion. Nor was it clear how God's camera had managed to take pictures of those characters who only functioned inside Jesus' parables — the widow with her coins, the unjust steward, the Pharisee and the Publican.

Still, there they all were, since this was a sacred book. It matched the black leather sacred one my mother and the preacher read. "With God," as she often said, "all things are possible."

As a counterbalance to Hurlbut, my father's parallel purchase was a bookcase that already contained cheap secular encyclopedias in the outer row and, in the row behind, Zane Grey, Edgar Rice Burroughs, Charles Alden Seltzer.

If she found me dipping into these cowboy secondaries, my mother would demand to know if I was reading any bad words there.

"No ma'am, and if I come to any, I'll skip," I said piously.

Besides, in those days very thick books were on sale at Penney's for 49 cents apiece. Since I was known in the extended family as a reader, by grade two my farmer kinfolk — who measured literature, like meat, by the pound — were giving me Walter Scott and Dickens.

Hurlbut remained the central, sacred book. I could not count how many times in childhood I read it straight through, plus extra rereadings of favorite stories, but even after these birthday classics, after a library card brought Nancy Drew into my life, long after I had been behind the sofa and allied myself with Jesse James and the Daltons, Hurlbut influenced me more.

With its phonetic spellings, Hurlbut taught me how to use a dictionary. My father could enjoy his radio after I learned to match words heard in Sunday School with those long and short vowels and accent marks. The stories had too few girls, but their range was wide: Delilah, Deborah, Jezebel, Ester, Rahab, Ruth, Jael. Even male heroes like David, Jacob, Peter made serious, costly mistakes. If virtue was often rewarded, sometimes it overlooked Jepthah's daughter, Job's first family. Justice could even turn mean for Ananias and Sapphira, or Uzzah, who had only touched that ark to steady it.

Hurlbut's Bible taught me the shape of urgent plot with serious issues at stake. It briefed me at a young age on the many biblical allusions to be later found in western literature. And it added to suspenseful story lines a dimension that the cowboy books did not apply to the cattle range or the canals of Mars. Though I could not have verbalized it then, Hurlbut convinced me that individuals mattered, their biographies were significant, their small lives passed under the eye of God, and that even a story could be a vessel for truth. No, not "could," but "should."

Yet the cowboy books taught me something, too. A love of action, landscape, animals; a preference for the kind of protagonist who takes things into his own hands. The pull between these two literatures can be seen in almost everything I have written since.

In time I wore out my Hurlbut, cracked its spine, had loose pages taped in everywhere. Then it disappeared.

Now in Chapel Hill, half a century later, I hoisted this copy, not the beautiful leather-bound edition that my mother could ill afford, but one uglier and tackier, with a stamped pea-green cover on which a pea-green young shepherd harpster, shod in yellow thong sandals, holding a yellow harp, wore on his waist a yellow pouch for his sling and five smooth stones. I thought of my father, of his eventual return to the church and long service there. As I opened the book, I thought of my own departure and return. I know neither one of us was ever free of questions.

I could not tell in which year this version had been issued, though the fuzzy pictures claimed to be printed from new plates, and a publisher's note said 200,000 copies had already been sold. The tan pages smelled musty, and none was underlined as mine had been.

But inside there was a real angel still speaking to Gideon on a real threshing floor, and a real Jesus lifting the cold right hand of the dead daughter of Jairus just before He told her to rise.

It cost four dollars. I bought it.

Doris Betts has taught writing at the University of North Carolina at Chapel HIll for 33 years. Her ninth book of fiction, The Sharp Teeth of Love, *will be published in the spring of 1997.*

Jerry Bledsoe

on

Reynolds Price's

A Long and Happy Life

JERRY
BLEDSOE
DAVID TERRY 8/96

I grew up in a house in which, to my memory, there were only two books: a Bible on an end table in the living room and a primitive sex manual with line drawings of vital secret organs hidden in a dresser drawer in my parents' bedroom. I guess I need not point out to which I was most drawn, or add that it was not the one likely to lead me to a lifelong appreciation of books.

Unfortunately, the only other books that appealed to me in childhood were comic books. Which may explain why I flunked English in high school. If I ever actually turned in a book report, you can bet that it came from a *Classics Illustrated.*

Soon after my hairbreadth escape from high school, however, I took a fateful first step that would eventually lead me not only to reading but to a virtual obsession with books. I joined the Army.

Although I enlisted on the promise that it would send me to art school (I wanted to be a cartoonist at the time), the Army chose to make me a writer (a word that I use in this case in its loosest definition). For a year I worked as a reporter on a post newspaper in Alabama, and in time I was assigned to Tokyo as a feature writer for a Korean propaganda magazine. Still I took little notice of books, unable, or unwilling, to recognize the vital connection between reading and writing.

Indeed, up to that point, I can recall reading only two books: a collection of syndicated columns by a man named Jim Bishop, recommended to me by the editor of the post newspaper, and, oddly enough, a book about J. Edgar Hoover and the FBI. I had sought out the latter after seeing my favorite actor, Jimmy Stewart, in *The FBI Story.* I had fantasies of becoming an FBI agent and marrying June Allyson, who had played Stewart's wife in a couple of earlier movies, but not in *The FBI Story* — although she should have.

Neither of these books had whetted an appetite for others, however, and I remained without a real hunger for reading until a cold and drizzly Sunday afternoon in the fall of 1962. Barely 21, I had already been in the Far East for a year and a half (Okinawa, Taiwan, Japan). I was desperately homesick and lonely. It must have been late in the month, with payday looming, because if I'd had money (my monthly pay as a PFC was $90), I surely would not have wandered into that military library on the outskirts of Tokyo. Clearly I was looking for distraction.

Just inside the entrance was a shelf of featured books, and the first in line, propped on a wooden stand, was small and unassuming, with an inconspicuous green and white cover. I have no idea what prompted me to pick it up. Certainly, it wasn't the recommendation on the cover by Eudora Welty, because I didn't know who she was. It couldn't have been the name of the author, Reynolds Price. This was his first book, and I had never heard of him, either. Maybe it was the title, *A Long and Happy Life*. I surely was miserable enough for any hint of happiness to attract me.

On the jacket flap I read that the story was set in North Carolina, and that, no doubt, was what prompted me to turn to Chapter One and read the first paragraph. It was a single sentence that went on for nearly a full page, more than 200 words long, flying in the face of everything the Army had told me about writing (short sentences, short paragraphs, simple statements): "Just with his body and from inside like a snake, leaning that black motorcycle side to side, cutting in and out of the slow line of cars to get there first, staring due-north through goggles toward Mount Moriah and switching coon tails in everybody's face was Wesley Beavers..." it began.

It sucked me up as a whirlwind might. Suddenly I

was back in North Carolina, seeing that black motorcycle weaving in and out of Mildred Sutton's funeral procession, Rosacoke Mustian spraddle-legged on the back, her skirt hiked up, clinging to Wesley Beavers, hiding her face against the hot wind and her own chagrin.

That was not my introduction to Rosacoke Mustian. I knew her already, or thought I did, only by a different name. I had become engaged to her back in North Carolina just before I left for Okinawa, and we had parted with vows of everlasting love and letters every day. The letters had come faithfully for several weeks, then I had been sent to Taiwan, where mail could not reach me, and when I returned three weeks later, eagerly anticipating a full mail sack, I hurried to the mailroom only to have the clerk shake his head — nothing. I thought he was playing a practical joke.

"Come on, man," I said, laughingly, "give me my mail,"

"If I tell you you've got no mail, you've got no mail," he said and turned to other matters.

Jolted, I retreated to my bunk to compose a tentative but beseeching letter. What was wrong? Was it because I'd been away on maneuvers and unable to write?

Weeks of agonizing silence followed before the dreaded answer arrived. She had met somebody else. She was sorry. She hadn't meant to hurt me. She'd like her class ring back.

Later, I heard that she'd been seen at the county fair with a guy with a duck-tail haircut who rode a motorcycle. Wesley Beavers, without question.

I checked out the book, hurried back to my barracks, sprawled on my bunk, and read it straight through. I was so caught up in it, so happy to be back amidst the places and people of my blood, that I missed our mess hall's once-a-month Sunday night supper of T-bone steaks.

The story was a simple one of a young woman's love for a young man who knew little of love, and soon I was pulling for Rosacoke, for she had a basic goodness and would never do what my Rosacoke had done. When she gave herself to Wesley Beavers completely, I knew that she was making a serious mistake, but I couldn't do a thing to stop her. And near the end, when he offered out of duty to take her to Dillon, South Carolina, for a quickie wedding, I was encouraging her decision to have this child alone, hold up her head and go on with her life, free of him at last.

But she postponed giving him a definite answer until after the Christmas pageant at Delight Baptist Church, in which she was playing Mary, and while she was trying to calm a fretful baby Jesus at her bosom, she had looked out into the audience, found the eyes of Wesley Beavers and decided that her answer would be yes after all.

And that was the end.

I put down the book that night worried that Rosacoke would not have the long and happy life for which she yearned so deeply. (It would be another 26 years before I found out whether she had, when Price brought out his seventh novel, *Good Hearts*.)

After I had settled back and begun to disengage myself from the people and places of *A Long and Happy Life*, I lay for a long time letting the wonder of what I'd just undergone wash over me. A book, mere words on paper, had snatched me up, delivered me home, spoken to me in familiar and comforting voices, entangled me so intimately in the lives of created characters that I had wanted to jump into the pages myself, shouting, "No, Rosacoke! Don't go with him, take me."

I sensed that I had undergone a transforming experience, and indeed I had, for I soon was back at the library, and before long I had discovered Mark Twain, Ernest Hemingway, John Steinbeck and Marjorie Kinnan Rawlings. The more I read, the more I wanted to read — and the more I began to dream of someday learning enough to create some transforming magic of my own.

I don't know know if I've accomplished that yet, but ironically, years later, I did write a book that to my disbelieving eyes attracted words of praise from Reynolds Price, whom I had never met. And, far too belatedly, I wrote to thank him — for more than he ever knew.

Jerry Bledsoe was a feature columnist for more than 20 years for the Greensboro and Charlotte newspapers. He won numerous awards including two National Headliner Awards and two Ernie Pyle Memorial Awards. He's the author of 13 books including Bitter Blood, *which became a TV mini-series, and* The Angel Doll, A Christmas Story.

Fred Chappell

---

on

Julia Child's

Mastering the Art of French Cooking

FRED
CHAPPELL
DAVID TERRY 8/96

I first began teaching at the University of North Carolina in Greensboro in the mid-1960s, and my salary was not princely. It could not claim any rank of nobility; in fact, it did not even ascend to the middle class. Our television set was a small black-and-white job that brought in the public broadcasting channel through a dancing veil of nervous speckles. Through the turmoil of this electronic squall we made out the commanding form of Julia Child as she boiled and sauteed, chopped and sliced, nattered and sweated. She was cooking food the way French people cooked it in France.

Our son Heath was six years old, and he adored the show. I was puzzled as to what so fascinated him about it, but I remember vividly how he once erupted into a waterspout of laughter and fell off the sofa in amazement. Julia had produced an enormous mallet and was smashing a turkey carcass to atoms. It came to me then that Heath saw the show as a one-woman sitcom.

There was indeed a great deal of accidental humor about it, though I think the usual rumors are untrue. We never saw Julia drop an omelet on the floor; she never brandished a vegetable at the camera and began her instructions with the direction, "First, take a leek."

Instead, she alerted a deep need that had been plaguing me for a long time. I had always thought that food could be interesting if one took a fine interest in it. My father, who had pursued a number of successful careers over his six decades, once confided that cooking was the most interesting work he had ever undertaken. Yet he was but a timid chef who specialized in chocolate fudge and charcoal-grilled steaks. As I watched Julia Child I became convinced that cooking was an art as satisfying as music or poetry, and employing methods equally arcane and difficult.

When I invested too much of my puny instructor's salary on a boxed two-volume set of books called, with vernal optimism, *Mastering the Art of French Cooking*, I realized just how arcane and difficult these methods were. I read straight through the first volume and well into the second, but I did not try my hand at any dish for three years.

As my wife, Susan, explained to me, there were some ground rules to be comprehended first, chief among them being that I must clean up — thoroughly — whatever messes I made. I agreed to this condition and tried to live up to it, but I managed to make a few messes so complex I had no clue how to undo them. Susan rescued me, with exasperated forgiveness.

At last I screwed up my courage and began with the easiest recipe I could find. This was *crepes de pommes de terre*, that is, grated potato pancakes. There were to be three for our dinner, and the recipe was sufficient for six if not eight people. But I hadn't confidence enough to change the proportions. We would have leftovers, I figured, not knowing that potatoes sauteed in butter become rancid within hours. The ingredients were simple and mostly accessible: 8 oz. cream cheese, 2 eggs, 2 1/2 lbs. grated potatoes, 6 oz. Swiss cheese, whipping cream, salt and pepper, etc. Fresh herbs like chives and chervil were called for, but parsley would have to do.

Amazingly, the dish came out all right. It was an elementary recipe and I followed it slavishly, even to the extent of taking a small handful of *gratinee* at a time and twisting it in a ball in the corner of a "scrupulously clean" dish towel to get out the moisture. Today I would stir in a tablespoon or so of seasoned flour (*sans* salt) to take up some of the water and be done with it, but in 1970 I didn't have the nerve. When the crepes were served, along with Susan's genuine and delicious main courses, my wife and our guest made complimentary noises, soothing murmurs, and I was quite pleased with myself, even though I found these potatoes bland in the extreme. Today I would add a rasping or two of nutmeg and a sprinkle of cayenne.

In fact, I would do a great many things differently. When I turn with fond nostalgia through the pages of these two handsome volumes, I feel as if I were looking at the cuisine of another century. Almost any recipe calls for pounds of butter, oozy gobs of whipping cream, cups of oil, gallons of veal or chicken stock. When I stopped smoking cigarettes some seven years ago, my love of food added 15 pounds to my no-longer-boyish frame, and a bad hip has prevented my exercising the excess off. But if I still ate according to the philosophy of *Mastering the Art of French Cooking*, I would have to be transported by tow truck and canal barge. Other considerations come into play, too. Susan and I object to the barbarities of factory farming and so eschew veal and chicken unless they are range-fed.

But it is unfair to carp at a style of cuisine introduced 30 years ago into a nation where by and large there was no style in cooking. Southern cookery has always been vaunted by us Southerners, yet except for that of Louisiana and the South Carolina low country it is vapid fodder. I collected Southern recipes for quite a while and found good ones for jambalaya and Hopping John, but otherwise it was chicken fried in a cornmeal crust, in a buttermilk crust, in an egg-white crust, even in a peanut-butter crust. Once I came across a recipe that I still regard as the epitome of ordinary Southern cooking. It was for a dessert: Coca-Cola cake.

So Julia and her co-authors (Louisette Bertholle and Simone Beck for Volume I, Beck for Volume II) had their work cut out for them. Over and over they emphasize how economical, even frugal, French cuisine is. They do so because most Americans, including myself, imagined French cookery to be dreadfully expensive. We probably got this notion from the movies that showed us actors in evening dress nibbling exorbitant pheasants while tippling Chateau

Rothschild or Dom Perignon. Also, these ladies insisted, this style of cooking was easy once you got the hang of it.

Well, so is tightrope walking, I'm sure, but it takes practice, and one of the first things that practice teaches about *Mastering* is that the procedures are unnecessarily complicated and can be simplified without harm by eliminating half or even two-thirds of the steps. Many of the recipes must be jettisoned also, unless clogged arteries are your idea of a good time. *Boeuf en daube* calls for 4 Tb. goose fat, 6 oz. blanched bacon, a split and blanched calf's foot, beef suet, and a 6-inch square of blanched pork rind; prosciutto is optional, but butter is needed for the vegetables. This might be a recipe, or it might be a list of necessaries for a Chevrolet lube job.

It is too easy to make fun of the clothes we used to wear, the music we used to listen to, the provender we used to munch. *Mastering the Art of French Cooking* gave us an alternative, it opened our eyes and altered our senses, it showed us that pleasure was to be taken in the kitchen as well as at table. And it helped to produce a whole generation of what just may be some of the best French cooks in the world: East Coast American housewives.

A great many of us owe Julia Child a great deal, and I am pleased to acknowledge my own debt — and not too proud to apologize here and now to the friends I have caused suffering through her influence.

Fred Chappell, native of Canton, has won several awards, including the Sir Walter Raleigh Prize and the Bollingen Prize for Poetry. His fiction includes I Am One of You Forever *and* Brighten the Corner Where You Are. *He is professor of English at the University of North Carolina at Greensboro. He also is book columnist for the* News & Observer. *He lives with his wife in Greensboro.*

Hal Crowther

on

Alan Paton's

Cry, The Beloved Country

DAVID TERRY 8/96
HAL CROWTHER

There is a lovely road that runs from Ixopo into the hills. These hills are grass-covered and rolling, and they're lovely beyond any singing of it.

Why did the opening sentences of *Cry, The Beloved Country* burrow into my memory and hold a place for 35 years, against the challenges of several thousand novels? "Call me Ishmael" is the only launching in English fiction as familiar to me as Alan Paton's solemn evocation of the green hills of South Africa. The words "lovely beyond any singing of it" persist and occur to me continually, while much of the great poetry I memorized has faded.

My guess is that these words stay with me because the book that followed rolled over me like an express train. I was 16 or 17 when I read *Cry, The Beloved Country*, still ranked by most critics as the great South African novel. Discounting some sportswriter's celebration of Roy Campanella or Willie Mays, it must have been the first book about a black man's life to get this particular white boy's attention.

Unquestionably it was the first book with race as its dominant theme. Race hadn't been much of an issue for me. In the rural Appalachian county in New York where I grew up, there couldn't have been a dozen African Americans. The only one I ever encountered was an elderly barber named Ken Bliss, who wasn't noticeably darker than the local Greeks or Sicilians.

My parents were teachers from the progressive college generation of the late '30s, liberal Republicans back when that was no contradiction. In their house I never heard the word "nigger" or any racist language. My parents were racial optimists, white people who rooted for Jackie Robinson and Joe Louis and loved the music of Duke Ellington and Count Basie. Nothing I knew had prepared — or prejudiced — my response to a novel about South Africa or a black character like the Rev. Stephen Kumalo.

Kumalo was an ambitious, even a defiant creation according to the politics of that time. In the novel, this elderly Anglican priest from a rural parish travels to Johannesburg to find a lost son whose name, of course, is Absalom. The search for the prodigal becomes a bitter education in the subtleties of "apartheid," an ordeal that tests his faith in God and human nature. When the son is arrested for the murder of a white engineer, a famous liberal and friend of black Africans, Kumalo's tragedy becomes the symbolic tragedy of a country where race has become the bleeding wound that no one can bind.

I don't remember how the book came into my hands. It was my father's, from the spare bedroom stacked with novels, biographies and histories that he ordered from publishers in New York (the nearest reputable bookstore was 75 miles away). I do remember that, for a child sheltered from all the ambiguities of racial conflict, *Cry, The Beloved Country* was like a trumpet sounding and a curtain rising to reveal some alternate reality.

In the nick of time. As a young man I was not only ignorant but experimenting with naive conservative ideas. (One of them, that most people will behave decently and generously without any pressure from the government, is a fable the civil rights experience ought to have discredited forever). When the marches and sit-ins began in the early '60s, I was still inexperienced and conservative. But by then I had read Paton, and I never doubted for an instant which side I would choose. Of all my political choices, that may be the only one I never questioned or reconsidered.

I recently met an Englishwoman, a BBC radio producer, who told me that Paton's book had also formed all her attitudes about race, long before she had any opportunity to test them. The humanity of Stephen Kumalo is so irresistible that no one could read the book and walk away from it still a racist, still committed to theories of racial superiority or racial separation. I still believe that. But most people who would save their souls with such a book will never read one. Racism is a strict religion, and ignorance is its first commandment.

When *Cry, The Beloved Country* was published in the United States in 1948, an American reviewer praised it as "the biography of a primitive human soul." A condescending reading, it seems to me now. Kumalo's dignity and decency make sophistication seem as irrelevant as race when it comes to the measure of a man. "Primitive" now sounds almost like a racial slur.

The measure of a great book and a great character is that they inspire us when we're innocent and amaze us when we're experienced. I remembered Kumalo as an honest country priest, a simple, humble old man staggering under a terrible sorrow. On a second reading I found him infinitely more complex — definitely not a plaster saint with an ebony varnish. We see him commit sins of pride, anger, deceit and vindictiveness. We know he has considered adultery. Kumalo's shabbiness is almost embarrassing to Jarvis, the white landowner; to his village parishioners, he cuts a distinguished figure.

His suffering, an old man's suffering, speaks compellingly to the older reader I've become. When I was a son who had never been a father, losing an only child who is hanged for murder was an agony quite beyond my imagination. There were also these words, to describe Kumalo: "Deep down the fear of a man who lives in a world not made for him, whose own world is slipping away, dying, being destroyed, beyond any recall."

That fear certainly resonates with me now, as the 21st century menaces me before I've really made my peace with the 20th. All our equations have changed. In the arrangements between its races, South Africa has changed even more drastically than the United States. Nelson Mandela, a prisoner serving a life sentence when Alan Paton died in 1988, is now president-for-life if he so chooses. The most visible African American leader was once a Christian minister named King, and now it's a Muslim minister named Farrakhan. A world all unfamiliar. But *Cry* is still the book I'd recommend to a 16-year-old, black or white, for whom I had very high hopes.

On its surface, it might strike him as old-fashioned. Paton's subtitle, "A story of comfort in desolation," sounds almost Victorian. Some of its sentiments are distinctly out of vogue, like this speech by Rev. Msimangu, the black intellectual who leaves the civil rights movement to take monastic orders: "I see only one hope for our country, and that is when white men and black men, desiring neither power nor money, but desiring only the good of their country, come together to work for it."

Alan Paton is as free of cynicism as any serious writer in our language. Like Stephen Kumalo, Paton was a devout Christian who later wrote a book of meditations on the prayers of St. Francis of Assisi. Like his novel's white martyr, Arthur Jarvis, he was an activist for racial justice. He founded and served as chairman of South Africa's interracial Liberal party, which was later banned by the government. Paton seems dated only because he's guileless, and most of us have become accustomed to a certain amount of guile in our fiction. *Cry, The Beloved Country* wears its heart on its sleeve.

For all that, it's a smart book — angry, clear-eyed and prophetic. When Msimangu, the thinker, predicts the corruption of some of the first blacks to win power, we see Winnie Mandela, as well as Americans like Marion Barry and Ben Chavis. Msimangu isn't warning whites so much as pleading for their attention when he says, "I have one great fear in my heart, that one day when they are turned to loving, they will find we are turned to hating."

That was written 50 years ago. It would be hard to improve upon it as a commentary on history that's still unfolding.

Cry, The Beloved Country embodies values that become more impressive the more you learn about the time and the place that formed them. It took me years to understand that Jim Crow was in many ways more repugnant than apartheid. American racists were part of a secure white majority, while white South Africans, outnumbered four to one, were justified in their fears of annihilation. From that angle, America's white liberals seemed to operate out of noblesse oblige and still expect gratitude; South Africa's worked against their own people and their own interests and expected nothing in return except consciences they could live with.

This was a group that included many of South Africa's best writers, Nadine Gordimer and Athol Fugard as well as Alan Paton. They weren't bargaining, these liberal whites trapped with the rest by Africa's inevitable transformation. They weren't maneuvering for advantage. Theirs was the kind of moral heroism that captures a boy's imagination and used to capture an occasional adult's.

They called themselves "Kaffirboeties." It was a term of derision in Afrikaans, meaning essentially "nigger-lovers," and they wore it with pride. In his introduction to *Cry, The Beloved Country*, Paton praises Professor R.F.A. Hoernle, a pioneering white liberal, as "prince of Kaffirboeties."

At an age when most boys wanted to be Mickey Mantle or Jack Kennedy, I discovered that I wanted to be Professor Hoernle. The book was entirely to blame.

Hal Crowther was born in Canada and arrived in North Carolina in the '70s. He has written for Time, Newsweek, *the* Buffalo News *and produces a syndicated column originating in the* North Carolina Independent. *He has a collection of essays titled* Unarmed but Dangerous *and has earned the H.L. Mencken Award, among others.*

Clyde Edgerton

---

on

Ralph Waldo Emerson

Cly Edger-
de Eton
DAVID TERRY 8/96

I was a high school sophomore whose life and death musings were tied mostly to the teaching of my Baptist church. What seemed most important in my moral universe had already happened: Christianity had been founded. Jesus had died for our sins. Saul had become Paul. Lions had fed on Christians. Now it was important to be good every day.

But being good was not much fun. Throwing spitballs in Sunday school was fun. Sunday school itself was dull duty.

Fun also came with hunting and baseball, and while growing up I was generally happy and secure knowing that I had all I needed: Mama, Daddy, home, friends, girlfriend, church, bird dog, shotgun, ball glove, a good throwing arm, and a smooth swing at the plate. My grades were average.

By the 10th grade I had decided to pass up on college and join the Coast Guard. I could see little need for more education. And although I'd never heard of "intellectual rebellion," I had begun to resist the same Bible stories told over and over with no stated application to modern problems.

I remember complaining about this to my mother. And yet I still felt the presence of good and evil — of God and the Devil — in my world, in spite of my vague notion that all the big Christian battles had already been fought centuries before.

And so, as I started reading another routine English assignment from my 11th-grade textbook one night, I was hit in the face by these words from the first paragraph of an essay called *Nature* written by somebody named Ralph Waldo Emerson: "The foregoing generations beheld God and nature face to face; we, through their eyes. Why should not we also enjoy an original relation to the universe? Why should not we have a poetry and philosophy of insight and not of tradition, and a religion by revelation to us, and not the history of theirs?... The sun shines today also.... Let us demand our own works and laws and worship."

My mind was set afire as if soaked in gasoline. Emerson had served me up a bowl of intellectual rebellion at just the right time in my young life. I, of course, knew nothing of Emerson's role in preparing for an American as opposed to an English-American literature. I knew nothing of Emerson's standing, or lack of standing, as a philosopher. I had some trouble taking in his general views. But those vigorous sentences! There in the third paragraph of my assignment, one started this way: "We are now so far from the road to truth, that religious teachers dispute and hate each other...."

"So far from the road to truth"? Was not this blasphemy?

But this man, this writer, was a believer, was he not? A believer could question "truths" handed down from his elders? And in the fifth paragraph, as if in the fifth room of an ancient ruin, I encountered this heavy gem: "If the stars should appear one night in a thousand years, how would man believe and adore; and preserve for generations the remembrance of the city of God which had been shown!" I read on hungrily, hoping, then knowing, that in every few paragraphs I would uncover a full, powerful sentence that I could roll in my mind, that would lead me ahead, searching for the next.

Here was a writer who wrote about ideas — ideas that heated my blood. He was moral, but not dictatorial and narrow. He was kind. He loved the world, and it seemed as if he had written some sentences for no one but me. For example, in those days I loved the outdoors, but didn't know how to say so creatively. There, three paragraphs later, Emerson told me that "Crossing a bare common, in snow puddles at twilight, under a clouded sky, without having in my thoughts any occurrence of special good fortune, I have enjoyed a perfect exhilaration. I am glad to the brink of fear. In the woods, too, a man casts off his years, as the snake his slough and at what period soever of life is always a child. In the woods is perpetual youth."

Nature pushed me out to the bookstore for my first purchase of a book unassigned: *The Portable Emerson*. My favorite essays became *The American Scholar* ("Meek young men grow up in libraries, believing it their duty to accept the views which Cicero, which Locke, which Bacon, have given; forgetful that Cicero, Locke, and Bacon were only young men in libraries when they wrote these books."); *The Divinity School Address* ("In the street, what has [the preacher] to say to the bold village blasphemer? The village blasphemer sees fear in the face, form, and gait of the minister."); and *Self-Reliance* ("See what strong intellects dare not hear God himself unless [God] speaks the phraseology of I know not what David, or Jeremiah, or Paul.")

I was taken by all this, especially by the essay, *Self-Reliance*. Emerson gave me a kind of fledgling confidence in my own words and thoughts, in my right to speak my mind. He led me, in turn, to Thoreau. And with my digestion of Emerson and Thoreau, a realization, a belief began to take shape in my 16-year-old mind. The belief was that "America" and "democracy" were not so much about accepting God as handed down to me by other humans; America and democracy were more than that. America and democracy had to do somehow with my being free to search for truth. I could think for myself.

I was so taken by the power of written words that by my senior year in high school I took a notion to go on to college, study English, then teach English literature so that I could spread the good news. This new route now would be as much fun as the Coast Guard would have been, I thought, and at the same time a little more open-ended, challenging. As for adventure out in the world, maybe I could join ROTC and become a fighter pilot for a few years.

I did go to college, joined ROTC, and studied English Education (secondary curriculum and instruction). But I stayed with Emerson. One night during my junior year, on the beach, I pulled out a book and flashlight and read from *Self-Reliance* to a startled girlfriend.

After college, during my stint as an Air Force pilot, I continued reading Emerson, but now I read Crane, Twain, Hemingway, Voltaire and Swift, too. My Air Force pilot friends wondered why I was interested in all this stuff. Later, back in graduate school, studying English Education, I met and fell in love with another English Education major; she led me to Faulkner, Welty and O'Connor. But in spite of these new writers under my belt, in spite of my own newfound inclination to write stories, I still had to read Emerson aloud, *Self-Reliance* — this time to my wife.

Years later, when a Baptist University withheld my teaching contract because of my own first novel, Emerson's *Self-Reliance* helped me listen to and act on my beliefs.

Then, a few nights ago, my wife read to me from the same essay. As I listened I remembered how the pages of the 11th-grade textbook looked — the headings, the print — and I remembered how the words on those pages helped me not only to listen, but to speak, not only to read, but to write.

Clyde Edgerton is the author of six novels, including Raney, In Memory of Junior *and* Redeye, A Western. *He has taught high school and college English and creative writing at St. Andrews College, Duke University, and Milsaps College in Jackson, Miss.*

Linda Flowers

---

on

James Agee's

Let Us Now Praise Famous Men

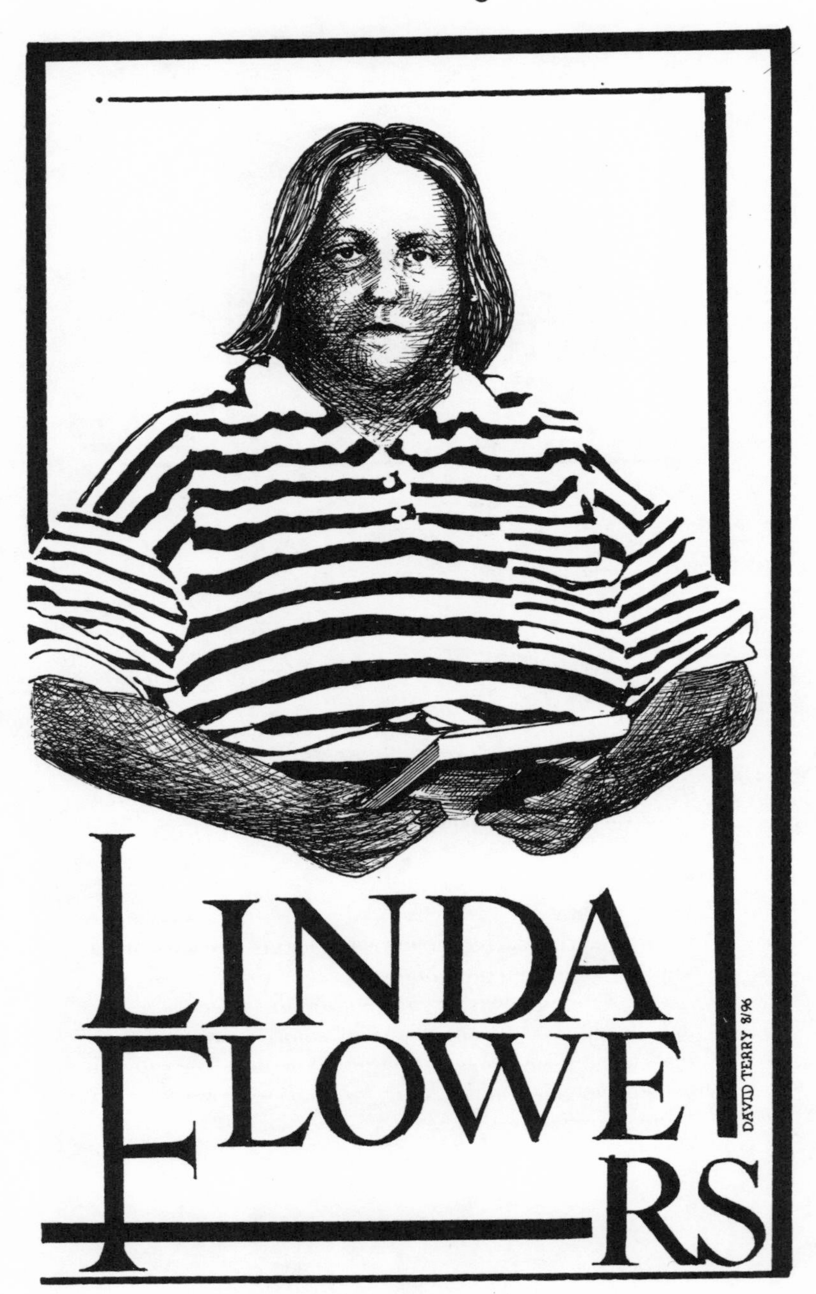
LINDA
FLOWERS
DAVID TERRY 8/96

Mama was ironing, and in my memory of that day in the first grade that I learned how to read, dark came early; a cold and blustery day, lonesome, the school bus pulling away as I ran inside.

"Well, read then," she told me. "That book there." Sliding the iron back and forth, no hurrying, no stopping, she pointed to one of my books (Dick and Jane and Spot, no doubt), and I rattled off the first lines of whatever it was.

I've not stopped since. Learning how to read was something. From the first, words leapt into my consciousness with fullness and power, and reading was as easy as walking the log across the ditch when I carried water to my father plowing in the lower field.

Growing up as an only child in the 1950s, my parents farming on the Faison land four or five miles out of town, in Duplin County, everybody I saw was always doing something. Boredom was as alien to us then as the notion nowadays that children should be entertained. If we weren't in the field, it was enough to sit on the porch and watch the cars pass by, or I'd get off by myself and read. Except for the Bible, however, there were few books. Yet every Saturday when he came home from town with the groceries, my father, when he had the money, would bring us each a magazine: for Mama, a *True Confessions* or a *Modern Romance*; for me, a funny book; for himself, a *True Detective*.

Along with my stacks of coloring books and the Sears catalog, such magazines (and sometimes *The Progressive Farmer*, *Grit* and the *Farm Journal*) were always a part of our household.

Shortly after I began teaching in Rocky Mount, my father, looking around my apartment at the many books shelved and stacked everywhere, declared, "Well, you kin shore read...if you can't do nothing else."

A very few books, however, I love too much to read: They may hurt too much, be too close to my own life and experience, ever to be read thoroughly, intently, and I know them only in luminous bits and pieces — but I know them, nonetheless. Most memorably, *Let Us Now Praise Famous Men*, James Agee's compelling, loving study of three tenant families in Depression-era Alabama.

Agee and the photographer Walker Evans worked for *Fortune* magazine in New York when, in the summer of 1936, they were assigned a photographic essay about cotton tenantry in the American South. The two simply loaded their car and set out. At a country store in Alabama a farmer invited them home with him, and for nearly two months Agee lived first with this tenant family, then with two others in the neighborhood. It is their lives that he describes in *Let Us Now Praise Famous Men*: the bone-wearying labor of raising cotton and nothing to show for it, the poverty, the deformations they endured of body and spirit, the children in whose eyes were neither hope nor expectation; and he describes, too, the feel of wood floors scoured with lye soap, your feet bare upon them, and the smell of the oil lamp as you go to bed, the beauty even of these pitiful houses, of the outlying barns and fields in moonlight.

The prose achieves such startling clarity that animals and people and the most common objects and odors and implements of life are forever caught, as if by a camera: hens "whose bodies end dirtily, like sheaves of barley left in rain"; a cow standing "in the shade, working her jaws, and suspending upon creation the wide amber holy lamp of her consciousness"; a "sockless and sweated foot in the fitted leathers of a shoe"; a wood porch "tender with rottenness...heavily littered with lard buckets, scraps of iron, bent wire, torn rope...those no longer useful things which on a farm are never thrown away"; and on and on.

For more than 400 pages, Agee would have us see

ordinary things as we have never seen them before. The rhythm of the prose builds and billows, carrying us along by sheer force, probing and pounding.

These three tenant families "live in a steady shame and insult of discomforts, insecurities, and inferiorities, piece these together into whatever semblance of comfortable living they can, and the whole of it is a stark nakedness of makeshifts and the lack of means." For this, Agree wants them to have our respect and understanding; and for the powers that are responsible for their lives, he invites our outrage and scorn.

Agee's words and Walker Evans' searing, unforgettable photographs were overwhelming to me 30 years ago when, a freshman at the University of North Carolina-Greensboro, I first came across this book. They still are.

Holding the book then in my hands, I knew I couldn't read it. Not all of it, not straight through. Agee's awe, his being so shocked, so impressed by these — to me — familiar people, these more or less familiar lives, embarrassed me. I knew enough trashy white people not to be taken in by them, as well as enough good country people not to find them unusual, either. Who were these tenants to be singled out? Why should they be in a book, when virtually everyone I loved was more or less their twin, and nobody had ever found us special?

I was a college freshman but I had still to learn that a book might be about me, that how I had lived, what my parents and their parents had seen and endured and confronted, was meaningful, too; that words were not just powerful (which I had always sensed), but might be personal. This was a lesson I was long in learning. Education was something that teachers had always implied would take me away, raise me up from my roots, and as a good student, I had taken this truth for granted — for it was and is a truth. That it is not the whole truth, however, was a lesson I had to shape and learn on my own. *Let Us Now Praise Famous Men*, on a day alone in the stacks of my college library, was like a hammer raised over my head: the dawning of a mere suspicion, a glimmer of knowing.

In the years since, I have seen more clearly the inherent dignity of my parents' lives: the satisfaction they took in labor well performed, in making the crops grow, in living simply. An outsider, Agee saw — and Walker Evans' pictures lastingly record — the beauty denied the familiar eye, as well as the breathtaking tragedy of the poverty, the brokenness of the lives.

A child of eastern North Carolina tenantry, I saw in Agee and Evans' book not just much that I knew already, but for the first time in my experience the effort of outsiders to make something of it: to behold and affirm, even to label as heroic a daily life that all of us simply took for granted; my family and our neighbors knew nothing else. Hardship and doing without were the way things were, and anybody worth his salt just kept going and did the best he could. So what else was new? Why make a book out of this? I asked that then — and a part of me asks it still. Wonderful photographs and fine words may enforce recognition, enable and sharpen perception, but they are not the thing itself.

As a professor now whose life is spent among books, and whose education and occupation are all about language, I understand that what *Let Us Now Praise Famous Men* really did for me was plant the seed that my own culture mattered; that it counted, too; that the eastern North Carolina I knew in my bones was as deserving of thought as *Hamlet*.

Writing waits upon perception and thinking, and because it shook me up, the book has made me do more of each — and, I am sure, do them better.

Linda Flowers teaches English at North Carolina Wesleyan College. Her study of eastern North Carolina culture, Throwed Away, *was published in 1990.*

Philip Gerard

---

on

William Styron's

Sophie's Choice

PHILIP
GERARD
DAVID TERRY 8/96

If you want to learn about people, take inventory of what they haul with them from place to place. For a summer during graduate school at Arizona, I worked as a long-haul moving man — a dozen weeks across 22 states. We were a two-man team: Dennis owned the rig and drove it under contract to North American Van Lines, and I was hired muscle. We ferried sofas and pianos, golf clubs and stereos, refrigerators and grandfather clocks. We hauled a solid marble table that weighed a thousand pounds and a rock garden that weighed two tons. Up the ramp went motorcycles, golf carts and once even the family car.

Still, from Phoenix to St. Louis, New York to Miami Beach, what we hauled was mostly junk — particleboard entertainment centers, rusted tools, lawn mowers that hadn't been started in years, couches with broken backs.

Late in the summer we picked up a load from a warehouse in Miami Beach — the bill of lading marked it "damaged in storage" — probably because some forklift operator had dropped the pallet box full of crates while trying to stack it. But we had no idea of the extent of the damage until we unpacked the crates at a ranch house in Las Vegas, Nevada. They contained not junk, but handmade antique furniture, heirloom china carried from Europe two generations before, handblown glass pitchers, crystal wedding goblets, original paintings. All were destroyed as thoroughly as if they had been deliberately vandalized.

The woman who received the shipment went into a kind of shock. She was attractive, mid-40s, with a good figure and carefully dressed blond hair. She spoke softly in clean sentences, and she carried herself with poise and dignity. She sat composed on her ruined sofa and handled each item we brought to her, and before long she was crying softly. She did not rant or curse us, as she had every right to do. She seemed to understand that we were not the kind of men who could have done this to her.

Now, as it happened, I was working on the moving truck because I, too, had lost nearly everything of material value that I owned. One night in Tucson, when I had left the house for exactly an hour, thieves had broken in and stolen my television, radio, stereo, my Martin six- and 12-string guitars, my new Stetson, even my manual Royal typewriter, a high-school graduation present from my parents, on which I had been writing my first novel — titled, with some irony, *Sanctum Sanctorum*. Holy of holies. The private, safe place. Without insurance.

The page in the typewriter platen had been stolen along with the machine.

That summer on the truck, I carried my manuscript — missing only its final chapter and the lost page — scribbling in truck stops and interstate hotel rooms, wrestling with the sentences in my head as the big diesel groaned along the highway, drowsing in the shimmer of sun on windshield, dreaming the thing to life.

While the woman cried over her things, Dennis got on the phone to the dispatcher to start the insurance claim. Even distraught, the woman graciously served us cold drinks. "They're only things," she said, slightly embarrassed. "It's not right to cry over things." When the insurance was all arranged, we apologized once more. She kissed us both and shook our hands warmly. "Thank you," she said, "for bringing my things to me."

On the way out, she touched my arm. "You look like a boy who reads," she said, handing me a paperback book she had just finished reading when we arrived. "Read this on your way to California." When we left, she seemed almost happy, almost relieved that the damage was so total and irrevocable.

The novel was *Sophie's Choice*, William Styron's

novel about people who are suddenly stripped of all their possessions — victims of the Nazi Holocaust. One of them, a Polish refugee named Sophie, survives Auschwitz with only her story, which she brings to America and gives to a young writer named Stingo in New York. The novel follows Stingo's fortunes as he labors to become a writer, as his fate becomes bound up with the doomed lives of Sophie and her volatile boyfriend, Nathan.

Like Stingo, I was "struggling to become some kind of writer." I, too, "yearned passionately to produce the novel which had been for so long captive in my brain." I, too, would wind up writing a different novel from the one I imagined I was writing.

Stingo learns the choice Sophie was forced to make at Auschwitz: If you can save only one of your children, which one will you save? Through Sophie's struggle with an unspeakable past, with her own survivor's guilt, Stingo finds the authentic passion no writer can do without.

As we pounded along the interstate toward Beverly Hills, I read on, feeling the sentences arc from page to page like one long current of electricity, and I understood not only something about loss, and about writing, but about writing the novel in particular.

A novel is about not knowing. That is the only knowledge a novel offers: that the world is an infinite mystery.

Stingo says it toward the very end of *Sophie's Choice*: "Someday I will understand Auschwitz," he had written in his diary. "This was a brave statement, but innocently absurd. No one will ever understand Auschwitz." The best he can do is ponder a life. "What I might have set down with more accuracy," Stingo then confides, "would have been: Someday I will write about Sophie's life and death, and thereby help demonstrate how absolute evil is never extinguished from the world."

The novelist is humble. His power, when he musters it, derives from not being sure, from questioning and probing, from tapping on the walls of his subconscious and listening with discipline for the echoes.

When I finished the book, I realized that the woman in Las Vegas had not been crying over broken crystal at all. She was crying, not for broken things, but for someone lost. Someone perhaps who had shared late suppers served on those china plates, who had sat with her on the Empire love seat and drunk champagne toasts out of crystal flutes as they admired their favorite painting.

Recalling a lost photograph in which she, a young girl, is seated with her mother at the piano, Sophie tells Stingo, "Now, somehow, just the memory of that photograph is a symbol for me, a symbol of what was and could have been and now cannot be."

What we had delivered to that beautifully proud woman in Las Vegas were only broken souvenirs. But she had a clear memory and a big heart, and in giving me the book she seemed to understand that I was the one who needed a souvenir.

A novel is, at its best, a profound souvenir — a remembrance — not just of real lives transformed into imaginary characters, but of life. Imagination fused with memory.

Over the years, I have returned to *Sophie's Choice* often in my thoughts. But I only recently reread it — after meeting William Styron at a lecture he gave in Charlotte. Over dinner, he talked about the importance of the novelist addressing public subjects — those events that happen right out there in the middle of a busy civilization, the hinges of history, the defining moments of a society — through the particular experience of a single, precious life, rendered with deep understanding.

It was a lesson I had already learned from his book, roaring along Interstate 15 at 65 miles an hour in an air-conditioned diesel, speeding toward the last chapter of my own first novel.

Gerard

Philip Gerard, a former newspaperman and freelance journalist, has been published in several magazines including New England Review/Bread Loaf Quarterly *and* The World & I. *He is the author of* Hatteras Light, Brilliant Passage, Cape Fear Rising *and* Desert Kill. *His essays have been broadcast on NPR's "All Things Considered" and he has taught writing for various events. He lives in Wilmington with his wife and enjoys sailing.*

David Guy

---

on

Ernest Hemingway

DAVID GUY
DAVID TERRY 8/96

I don't remember the title of the book that changed my life, and I'm afraid I can't even name its author. It was a cheap popular biography of Ernest Hemingway, a mass market paperback, thrown together rapidly, I suspect, around the time of his death.

The year I read it was 1963, two years after his suicide, but still before his own posthumous memoirs, A.E. Hotchner's notorious *Papa Hemingway*, or Carlos Baker's authorized biography. I had seen the book on my father's shelf for months, and when I had to do a book report on an author's biography for school, he suggested I read it.

I have an idea that Hemingway was one of my father's heroes. He was, like my father, the son of a physician in an upper middle class community, and had famously fled that background for a Bohemian life in Paris. My father had also wanted to be a writer, but buckled under pressure from his father and became a doctor.

That decision may have brought about his early death; he had by 1963 been suffering from leukemia for four years, would die of it a year later, and believed he had contracted the disease from the leaking radiation equipment that dermatologists used in the early years.

He had remained a great reader, though, and had moved beyond Hemingway, and was reading through Faulkner with great zest in that last year of his life. From his hospital bed, I remember, where he lay thin and weak, incredibly pale, he tore out a page from a Faulkner paperback with the titles checked off that he had already read.

"Get any of the others, Davy," he said. There were only three titles that weren't checked. The bookstore was down a hill from the hospital. I would have the books back to him that same afternoon.

The boy who trudged down the hill from the hospital was overweight, quiet, withdrawn, bewildered by his father's illness, desperate to succeed at something, to find a place in the world, to be a man. I believed that my salvation would come as an athlete, and spent hours of my free time with sports magazines, reading the same articles over and over as if they were holy writ. My father was frustrated that I didn't read better things, both because it would do me good and because reading was such a great pleasure to him. Suggesting that biography may have been a strategic move on his part.

The writer it portrayed was strictly the Hemingway of myth, the big game hunter and fisherman, expert boxer, occasional brawler, the barroom talker and legendary drinker, the companion of famous and glamorous women. Only later would I discover that the story was more complicated: Hemingway staged most of his boxing matches with smaller men he knew he could clobber; his serious alcoholism undoubtedly contributed to his deep depressions and to his suicide; his stories of romantic conquest were mostly boozy inventions; he seemed to have had a pathological obsession with killing that only ended when he put the gun to his own head.

No matter: The mythical Hemingway was the man I was interested in. He had succeeded where I wanted to succeed. And he had done so through writing.

Hemingway's work existed in a uniform Scribner's edition, and I was soon saving my money to buy those beautiful hardbacks, first the stories, starting with *In Our Time*, later *A Farewell to Arms* and the other novels. I was much taken with the Hemingway hero, the disillusioned, stoical, cynical man who had seen so much of life, starting with the Nick Adams of the early stories and going all the way to Colonel Cantwell in *Across the River and into the Trees*. I was attracted to this hero's manly stoicism. I hoped to develop that virtue to face the various disappointments and catastrophes of my own life, particularly my father's death.

Yet beneath that blustery surface was something else, and I believe it was the real gift that Hemingway gave me. I had discovered even at that age that I enjoyed the process of writing. I was fascinated by the way that playing with language could change meaning, create meaning, convey an impression or mood. I thought that was a private, minor interest of mine, but here was a writer — you could see it in every line — who was obsessed with the same thing, who practiced the craft of writing as surely as a woodworker practiced carpentry.

The Hemingway persona itself was largely a creation of language, of brilliant descriptive technique and a hypnotic use of dialogue. Hemingway was an extremely manly man — not an aesthete — who had made this vocation into a life's work. I began to think I might try to do the same thing.

There would be much future disillusionment with my hero, though I have not thereby become a Hemingway basher. I still regard him as a great writer and a fascinating man, with much more depth than he ever showed in his writing. But I will always be most grateful to him for showing me that my private interest in the workings of language could be made into the vocation of a lifetime.

David Guy is the author of four novels, including The Autobiography of My Body. *He has written articles for various magazines including* Tricycle, New Age Journal *and the* New England Review. *He has reviewed books for* The New York Times, The Washington Post *and* USA Today, *as well as being book columnist for the* News & Observer. *A graduate of Duke University, he lives in Durham with his wife.*

William McCranor Henderson

on

John Dos Passos'

The Big Money

BILL
HENDERSON

I think there was something about the title. *The Big Money*. It promised tough guys, sleek women, high stakes on the big board of life — the kind of reading that beguiled me the summer I turned 14. I was a balky adolescent, craving a wider world than the drowsy little Chapel Hill of those days, but too young to take one of the traditional escape routes: the pilgrimage to Mexico, the hitch in the Navy, the one-way bus to New York City.

I had been the kind of reader a literate parent despairs of: a nonreader. I believe the only grown-up book I had finished was *The Whip Hand* (my kind of title), written by a neighbor. I don't remember the plot, but the main character (a short, tough, hard-drinking Yankee, kind of like our neighbor) hogged the action in lush penthouses and savage corporate boardrooms, and there was a good bit of rough sex (to the degree that rough sex was permitted in the pulp fiction of the '50s).

That summer, my mother and I were sailing to Scotland to visit relatives, but I wasn't going to let it broaden my horizons. The way I saw it, I was being deprived of what I really needed, a summer hanging out in the empty streets, pretending I was James Dean. Apron strings, at such a crucial juncture, were crushing to my self-image. On the New York leg of our journey, I experimented with denial, re-inventing myself in my mind as an existential loner, goateed, cigarette dangling from mouth, destination the Left Bank of Paris. But it's next to impossible to get that *On the Road* feeling when you're cruising with your mom.

Ocean travel then had none of today's Carnival Cruise hilarity. Besides the shuffleboard tournament, high tea and dice-driven "horse racing" after dinner, there wasn't much to do on a Cunard liner but recline in deck chairs or habituate the bar (which, even in international waters, I was too young to do). I knew from prior voyages that having to wait eight or 10 days to get there was going to drive me crazy. Aside from the daily movie, the entertainment would be "square." The on-board library would be shabby and dull. I needed a good book — which, for me, meant a good title. During a last-minute drugstore stop before boarding ship, I found it: *The Big Money*.

I had no idea who John Dos Passos was, but his name had a promisingly gangsterish ring to it. I remember lying in my upper bunk, before the ship had even embarked, listlessly thumbing the pages, on the hunt for some good B-movie action. What I found instead weaned me instantly and forever from literary cheap thrills. Here, in a book, it seemed, the wider world I hankered after was opening up in my hands like a miraculous holographic pageant.

The Big Money wasn't the kind of book I had any experience with at all. Comparing it to *The Whip Hand* would be like lining up a Maserati next to a 10-speed Schwinn. It wasn't a single story but a majestic quilted pattern of American lives, some made up, some not. The main characters were fictional but so vividly drawn that they seemed to be walking around inside my head: Charley Anderson — Midwestern farm boy turned World War I ace, who made a fortune in aviation but couldn't shake his fatal restlessness; Margo Dowling — pretty, feisty, growing up abused, yet parlaying her chances into stardom on the silent screen; Mary French — sensitive, upper middle class, drawn to leftist social action only to see her spirit burn out in the aftermath of the Sacco and Vanzetti debacle.

Their narrative was interlaced with biographical vignettes of other American dreamers: Henry Ford, Isadora Duncan, Rudolph Valentino, Frank Lloyd Wright, William Randolph Hearst — the real nestled alongside the not-real, yet so naturally that, for me, the interchange between life and art vanished.

Dos Passos saw a brassy, hustling, unkempt America in the '20s, and somehow he got it all — the promise and the curse of it — on the page: farm, highway, factory, finishing school, lower class, upper class, suburb, city — rendered with a *savoir faire*, a "hipness" that in my state of puppyhood I found spectacular. Who was this Dos Passos guy? How did he know so much? Not just facts, but how real people behaved, in the shimmer of their public being and the aching privacy of their solitude as well:

"The young man walks fast by himself through the crowd that thins into the night streets; feet are tired from hours of walking; mind is a beehive of hopes buzzing and stinging; muscles ache for the knowledge of jobs, for the roadmenders' pick and shovel work, the fisherman's knack with a hook when he hauls on the slithery net from the rail of the lurching trawler. The young man walks by himself, fast but not fast enough, far but not far enough. One bed is not enough, one job is not enough, one life is not enough. At night, head swimming with wants, he walks by himself alone. No job, no woman, no house, no city."

I would later encounter a phrase about D.W. Griffith's *The Birth of a Nation*: "history written with lightning." This was how I experienced Dos Passos' book. To me, the product of a modest North Carolina school system, "history" was dead-boring, something to be avoided, the effluvium of state education committees. But this was history as I'd never encountered it before. And "creative writing," too, swirled into it like the rich dark chocolate of a marble cake.

Much later, struggling to be a novelist myself, I would return to *The Big Money* again and again, studying it — even copying out sections of it by hand — in particular, "Charley Anderson" and "Margo Dowling" — to watch the magician's hands at work and try to plunder his secrets. For what it's worth, I now know (as teachers do) how to label and classify what Dos Passos was up to. I can open the book for a student and point out the way he uses imagery to do heavy-duty work with effortless grace. I can trot out terms like "narrative texture" or "circumstantial summary" to categorize his means. But no analysis can come close to recapturing my raw amazement and delight with a book that made me feel, for the first time (as only an adolescent can), that I could get my hands around all America.

I don't recall much more about that voyage. Even when it occurred to me that I was reading the third book of a trilogy, *USA*, I didn't care. It seemed irrelevant because, all by itself, *The Big Money* had abducted me. In a quantum leap, I had left teen pot-boilers and pungent titles behind and was roaming the higher mountains of narrative imagination, from which I would emerge ready to read the way I would try to read the rest of my life: for keeps.

William McCranor Henderson has been a film-maker, rock musician, radio producer, freelance journalist, screenwriter and fiction writer. A Charlotte native, he has taught at North Carolina universities, most recently at N.C. State. His two novels are Stark Raving Elvis *and* I Killed Hemingway. *He is at work on a third plus a memoir of his recent stint as an Elvis impersonator.*

Fred Hobson

---

on

W.J. Cash's

The Mind of the South

FRED
HOBSON
DAVID TERRY 8/96

We were heading west in a 1957 Pontiac, on old Route 10 between Fargo and Bismarck, North Dakota, when I first opened W.J. Cash's *The Mind of the South*. It was early June 1964, and we were going to Oregon to work in pea canneries, where the money was supposed to be good and the working and living conditions (migrant camps) interesting — and where, after a couple of months of work, we could take off to see the rest of the West.

A decidedly literary tone had been established back about Indiana by my fellow travelers, rising juniors and seniors at Davidson College, a somewhat affected bunch, I thought, given to smoking pipes and listening to classical music. (I went to Carolina and was late coming to such refinements.) In any case, one particular Davidsonian, deep into Faulkner, lent me his Cash.

The whole trip, in fact, had been inspired by a rather self-indulgent cult of experience to which all of us subscribed, a creed best expressed by the quotation from Oliver Wendell Holmes Jr. (clipped, in fact, from the editorial page of the Raleigh, N.C. *News & Observer*) that I had kept on my bedroom wall all spring: "A man must share the action and passion of his times at peril of being judged not to have lived." That was powerful stuff and, along with Steinbeck's *Grapes of Wrath*, Holmes' creed sent us west.

The problem, of course, was that we were headed in the wrong direction. The nation's action and passion in 1964, it was already becoming evident, was to be found not in the West but in the South we were leaving behind, and that may explain why all of us were reading Faulkner and Styron and Ralph Ellison and Flannery O'Connor and a new novelist named Reynolds Price.

Even then I was aware of the ironies of heading to Oregon. The week before I had read that Northern and Midwestern college students were about to gather at Oberlin College in Ohio, preparing to head south to work in voter registration, deep into darkest Mississippi, into a long hot summer. Driving out of Dixie, just when the eyes of the nation were focused on it, was not a likely beginning for someone who had a vague idea of becoming a student of Southern culture and literature.

One thing we would all have in common that summer is the Yankees coming South and I heading North and West was reading W.J. Cash. *The Mind of the South* had gained a reputation as a guidebook for Northern civil rights workers bound for the Heart of Darkness, and I, having just heard of Cash, was also ready to dig in.

I had heard of him in George Tindall's Southern history class at UNC that spring and was fascinated by what I had been told of this shy, insecure Carolina newspaperman who had labored for nearly a decade and a half on the only book he was ever to write, and then shortly afterward (in 1941), having seen it published to great acclaim, committed suicide. I had just read Faulkner's *Absalom, Absalom* and *The Sound and the Fury* and was intrigued by the fictional Quentin Compson, who also committed suicide after telling his truth about the South. Cash, I decided, must have been a real-life Quentin.

That — and what was about to go on in Quentin's Mississippi — is why I began reading *The Mind of the South* as I headed across the Plains and the Rockies. I got barely a quarter of the way through the book, however, on the trip itself — it was a big book after all, and meaty, and there was driving to be done and Montana to be seen — and I didn't finish it until a couple of weeks later, when I was passing time on a somewhat slack graveyard shift, in the warehouse of Umatilla Canning Co. in Milton-Freewater, Oregon.

I was a prime candidate for Wilbur Cash, I realized even then, one ripe not so much for conversion as for some serious consciousness-raising. Up until that point I had been what is now considered an almost extinct species, a Southern liberal: What else, it seemed, was anyone in Chapel Hill in those days? I had been raised to revere Frank Porter Graham, my father's hero and former teacher, and I had supported the civil rights movement, although I had not, to any great extent, participated in it. Two years before, in fact, as a freshman — and a member of the Carolina freshman basketball team — I recall being mildly irritated by civil rights demonstrators who carried their protest from Franklin Street to Woollen Gym and made it difficult for fans to get in for a Saturday afternoon game with Wake Forest.

It would be flippant to say that Cash made the South as important as basketball to me, or invested it with the same sort of drama. But how the man could write! What struck me right off as I read him was not so much what he said as how he said it: He made language perform, made it dance and strut, as I had thought only writers of fiction could.

But he also told the truth, mainly, it seemed to me then and it still does. Cash wrote that the South, despite its internal differences, was "not quite a nation within a nation, but the next thing to it"; that the cavalier tradition of the Old South had been fraudulent; that the much-touted Southern aristocracy had also been largely fraudulent, at least outside the Tidewater; and that the "culture" and literature of which the earlier South had boasted was largely fraudulent as well.

Cash, that is, was the great demythologizer. He also had a penchant for the memorable term or phrase which, in fact, often said nothing new but said it in such a way that it stuck forever: the "proto-Dorian bond" stood for that solidarity of all Southern whites against blacks; the "savage ideal" for that code by which white Southerners suppressed dissent and punished dissenters. This met the truest test of social commentary or historical interpretation: The reader wants to leap up and exclaim "That's right!"

Here was no dry scholarly description of Southern religion; rather, here was religion described as a force designed "to draw men together in hordes, to terrify them with Apocalyptic rhetoric, to cast them into the pit, rescue them, and at last bring them shouting into the fold of Grace." And the worship of Southern woman Cash called "downright gyneolatry": "She was the South's Palladium, the shield-bearing Athena gleaming whitely in the clouds, the standard for its rallying, the mystic symbol of its nationality in face of the foe. She was the lily-pure maid of Astolat and the hunting goddess of the Boetian hill. Merely to mention her was to send strong men into tears — or shouts."

Cash, then, gave me a historical context for what was going on around me — made me realize, for example, why a psychology professor of mine had been beaten and urinated on (by one of Dixie's goddesses, one of its shield-bearing Athenas) when he protested segregation at a Chapel Hill restaurant, and why other Southern whites were committing all kinds of atrocities to prevent racial integration. It was Cash's savage ideal at work, his proto-Dorian bond asserting itself.

Since then — many years since — I've come to see the flaws in *The Mind of the South.* Cash generalizes outrageously; he neglects the South of Jefferson and Randolph, the intellectual life of an old South that was not quite so beknighted as he suggests; he writes not of the mind of the South but rather the mind of his *own* South, primarily the Carolina Piedmont, and exclusively the white South, the white male South. Finally, he writes not of "Mind" at all (since, Cash suggested, the South essentially had no mind) but rather the temper, the personality, of the South.

I am familiar with these complaints, and have voiced many of them myself. Still, I can't leave Cash behind, and not only because, even more than Faulkner, he awakened my deep interest in the South. There was no better time for me to encounter Cash than the summer of 1964, freedom summer, Mississippi summer, the summer of the slain civil rights workers, Goodman, Chaney and Schwerner — the summer when those very Southern atrocities Cash had identified and explained were playing themselves out again before the eyes of the nation. The ideal time, then. And, curiously enough, there was probably no better place for me to encounter Cash than in a small town in Oregon, lily-white and oblivious to the racial tensions of the Late Confederacy, a town 2,500 miles away from the Southern drama, where my own Southernness announced itself to me as it never had back in Dixie.

Fred Hobson is a professor of English at the University of North Carolina at Chapel Hill. His acclaimed biography of H.L. Mencken was published in 1995.

Janet Lembke

---

on

Thomas Bulfinch's

The Age of Fable

JANET
LEMBKE
DAVID TERRY 8/96

The kindhearted question asked of anyone who moves to a small Southern town is, "What church do you go to?" So, when I returned, after decades elsewhere, to the Shenandoah Valley town where I'd gone to grade school, taken ballroom dancing lessons, reached puberty and first fallen in love, the question was instantly posed. When I hedged, people stopped asking me directly. Instead, they pestered my mother.

"Oh," said my mother, a pleasantly devout woman, "she believes in Zeus."

I first met Zeus under his Roman name, Jupiter, and the encounter took place in the days of World War II. While my father served in the Army, my mother took herself and children south to live with her widowed mother for the duration. My grandmother's house was filled with books, books on the shelves of her secretary, books in breakfronts, books in stackable Wernicke cases that were supposed to have glass doors but didn't. They weren't the latest books — those came from the public library — but old ones, well-read, including all of Booth Tarkington's Penrod stories, Charles Kingsley's *Water-Babies*, George MacDonald's *The Princess and the Goblin*, a rainbow of the fairy tales collected by Andrew Laing, and L. Frank Baum's Oz books, first editions as it turned out, that had been given to my mother when she was a little girl.

It was Thomas Bulfinch who introduced me to the Olympians. One day in my 10th year, I took his *Age of Fable* from a living room bookcase and began to read. What divine adventures, what immortal quirks, lay revealed on those pages! I learned — then and later — of Juno's wrath at Jupiter's philandering, Dido's incendiary passion for Aeneas, and the delays caused by monsters and seductive nymphs as Ulysses strove to return home after the Trojan War.

Bulfinch certainly added much useful information to my small knowledge of sex. To guard my innocence from such seamy matters as adultery and illegitimacy, my grandmother regularly glued together the offending pages of *Life*, *Collier's* and the many other magazines to which she subscribed. She saw no need, however, to censor time-hallowed classics. In Bulfinch I read about everything from *grands amours* to cheating, with my mind's eye creating fabulous illustrations out of his lush Victorian language. There, along with Prosperine's fair body, Pluto quite ravished my imagination — that's Bulfinch's word, "ravish." There, with Latona, I lost virgin dignity (yes, his term); with Syrinx, evaded Pan's goatish lust; with Dido, raged and perished.

Along with furnishing sex education, Bulfinch helped me find patience. I yearned to be grown-up enough to study Latin, the enchanted language from which Bulfinch had transported many of the tales now holding me in thrall. English could only give a pale image of the old stories; If I wanted the whole zesty truth I had to know Latin. Such study, alas, was reserved for high school students. From my lowly position in the sixth grade, I read and gratefully re-read *The Age of Fable*.

The age for high school arrived soon enough, along with several serendipities. The first was a Latin teacher with a zest so contagious that I went on to major in classics. Later, when I'd become wife and mother, some demon directed my hand to pick up dusty college notes on even dustier archaic Latin. The results: a book of English poems based on the ancient lines and an invitation to act as the poet in a poet-scholar team translating Greek tragedy.

Four translations later, the spell cast by myths remains. During the last 10 years, I've lived in a near-wilderness on the shore of North Carolina's wide and salty river Neuse. Here I spend my days with fish, birds, plants and write essays not just about them but about the myths that spin overhead in the stars and hide within scientific names. (Look! That osprey was once king of Athens; that woodpecker, a prince who spurned a nymph's love.)

Believing in Zeus? Not exactly. But I'm off on a quest through the underbrush on the river shore and the classical underbrush in my head. Looking around, consulting the ancient writers to whom Bulfinch enticed me, I search for guidelines to proper human conduct amid the welter of everything else. And oh, the vanished Greeks have left behind a usable principle: Kairos — moderation, balance, a tender step on the earth, a soft hand on all we touch.

Bulfinch wrote that the gods of Greece and Rome "are too closely connected with the finest productions of poetry and art, both ancient and modern, to pass into oblivion." Decorating his tales with lines from such poets as Milton, Keats and Byron, he could not imagine otherwise. I can. His book, first published in 1853, is available today, however, in half a dozen editions. Investing in a copy is guaranteed to keep alive a host of allusions and to burnish a child's imagination until it gleams.

Yes, more modern mythologies exist. Robert Graves' versions are especially useful (despite his tangled way of telling stories) because he gives precise citations of the original sources. But Bulfinch is my mainstay. I never put *The Age of Fable* back in my grandmother's bookcase. That 1897 edition is bound in gold-emblazoned dark green cloth, with the name of the grandfather I never knew and the date 1904 inscribed on the inside front cover. Never mind that the binding is frayed around the edges, or that the glossy pages have become so brittle that they break at a careless touch. I keep it with me: a talisman.

Janet Lembke is a natural historian and language translator. Her latest book, Shake Those 'Simmons Down, *is a tribute to Southern trees and tree lore. She lives part-time on the banks of the Neuse River.*

William E. Leuchtenburg

---

on

Jonathan Daniels'

A Southerner Discovers the South

William
E.
Leuchtenburg.
DAVID
TERRY 8/96

When as a 15-year-old New York City boy in the 1930s I learned of Jonathan Daniels' *A Southerner Discovers the South*, I had small knowledge of the South and even less experience. My only encounter, if it can be called that, had come a few years earlier when I was 12 and had scraped together enough money tutoring kids in the neighborhood to take off by myself on a nine-hour Greyhound bus trip for three days in Washington. There, I had made a point of walking across Memorial Bridge and setting foot on the other side of the Potomac, so that I could say that I had touched down in the Southland, that mysterious country that had broken away in 1861 and both was and was not my own.

The notions of the South I had culled from film and radio had left me bemused. Movies such as *I Was a Prisoner from a Chain Gang* taught that it was a dark and fearsome place, stewing in injustice. I had also though, imbibed the quite different impression that below the Mason-Dixon line dashing blades and elegant ladies pursued memories of the Lost Cause with infinite grace.

I owe my introduction to *A Southerner Discovers the South*, a book that has had an enduring influence, to my family's odd taste in newspapers. Six days a week the only paper that entered our tiny apartment in the borough of Queens was the *Daily News*, the country's largest circulation journal. Since neither of my parents, both of whom had been raised in Hell's Kitchen on Manhattan's west side, had ever spent a day in high school, their choice of a tabloid with lots of pictures and juicy gossip made good sense. But on Sundays, unaccountably, my father always sent me to the local candy store to buy the foremost organ of the Re-publican Party, *The Herald Tribune*, a publication more usually found in a Park Avenue penthouse.

The *Trib* was an eye-opener. With my weekday chums confined to quarters in their church clothes, Sundays stretched on interminably, and I made the best of them poring over the sections devoted to sports, to the concert hall, and, above all, to books. And there on July 17, 1938, the *Herald Tribune's* book section carried a front-page review by the North Carolina journalist Gerald Johnson, under the banner headline: "Here is the Best Book on the Modern South."

A Southerner Discovers the South, a book I soon got hold of, recounts the 3,000-mile motor trip that Daniels, the well-regarded editor of Raleigh's *News & Observer*, took in the late spring and summer of 1937, early in Franklin D. Roosevelt's second term. Daniels appears to have headed off with certain questions vaguely in mind: How much was the South still a captive of the past? How well were the New Deal experiments working? But his venture was more particularly, as the title implies, an endeavor to "discover" his own land, with the reader, as unseen passenger in the car, invited to tag along.

Daniels started out where I had two years earlier — at Memorial Bridge — but his trek took him ever so much farther than I had gone: west as far as Hot Springs, Arkansas, and as deep into Dixie as the Florida peninsula. He chatted with governors and professors, union leaders and industrial magnates, who told him "solemn things, true things maybe." But he also listened, to "hitchhikers and tenant farmers,...hillbillies and Delta planters,...Syrians in Vicksburg and Cajuns in Louisiana," and "a lovely, starry-eyed, aristocratic young woman in love with a liquor salesman." Daniels found counterparts of 19th-century Memphis figures in the ornate lobby of the Peabody Hotel: "the slim brown planter in his linens, the erect colonel and his erect lady, the soft-handed gambler, the soft-breasted prostitute and the almost indistinguishable young matron, the bony little girls like bright identical beads and each a belle come to carnival." This was a land, I resolved, I was going to get to know.

To a degree, Daniels' book confirmed my split vision of the South. Daniels called his native section "the ill-kept back yard of America" and said, "The Old South in New Orleans is dying like a mansion turned to sleazy boarders." But he also wrote of "dogwood growing from a field of red clover," of "a sluggish stream full of white geese," of cattle "knee deep in the wide coastal meadows under the pecan trees," and church bells in Vicksburg "as full of sweet noise as Perugia at vespers."

Most of the book, however, challenged my simple conceptions of darkness and light. A road "greenly skirting the Cotton Kingdom," he noted, ran on "under royal palm, past pines cut for turpentine, past mimosas in bloom, past a fat blonde woman smoking a cigarette on the roadside and into Mobile through which so many bales of cotton have gone from the limited labor of lazy men to the world."

Daniels commented on the Tennessee Valley Authority's model town, which I idealized as the Utopia of a planned society: "After my first seeing of Norris, [Tennessee,] I hated it," for it was "a town without a cemetery, a town created without pain." He identified neither with those who denounced the TVA nor with those who came to "ooh and ah at the new heaven in the old earth," for he expected "to find in Eden both fruit and snakes."

Yes, the prose is a bit overripe, but it also stirred a young reader to think that the South was no simple place, that one needed to study its past to comprehend its present, that there were mysteries to explore.

As I reread the book now, I am disturbed by the extent to which the author's attitude toward African Americans was patronizing, sometimes worse, but I also understand why he was regarded as one of the South's foremost liberal editors.

Alas, he was capable of writing of "pot-bellied

pickaninnies" playing in the Arkansas dirt, of "Negresses black as licorice" in Mississippi, of "gangling earth apes" on Beale Street. Yet the passage that has been etched in my mind more than any other all these years, because as a provincial New Yorker with set notions of the ineradicable racism of Southern whites I was not expecting it, is of a very different sort. When a young woman, "the very picture of a Southern girl" in her crisp dress and immaculate coiffeur, informs the visiting editor of how she told a black servant who was not appropriately deferential, "Nigger, you get out of my house, and if you ever see me again you start running the minute you see me," she is unruffled, but, Daniels writes, "as [a] Southerner I was as shocked as if she had smashed a mirror with an ax."

On that summer morning in 1938 as I read the *Trib*, I had no way of knowing that one day I would be called on to review another of Daniels' books for the Sunday *New York Times*; that I would be invited to deliver the commemorative lecture in Louisiana on the occasion of the 50th anniversary of the assassination of Huey Long; and that, with my wife, I would, more than half a century later, make a voyage of discovery of my own through the South, heading down the Carolinas and Georgia to dip into the Florida Panhandle and pursue the Gulf Coast through Mobile and Biloxi and up the Mississippi to Baton Rouge.

I found aspects that Daniels would readily have recognized — a Confederate monument in every town square — but also a much changed South, now prospering as it had not in the eighth year of the Great Depression, and paying no nevermind to blacks and whites together at barbecue restaurants. After delivering a set of lectures at Louisiana State, I returned through the Alabama mountains and Chattanooga to Murphy and home.

"Home," the least expected development of all. In 1982, after 30 years of teaching at Columbia University, I had decided to abandon New York to spend the rest of my days in the South. A number of influences led to the decision. But the inclination to explore and settle in another land began the day I came upon a passage in Daniels' book where an obscure Arkansas country lawyer, his shelves lined with volumes on farm tenancy, inquires whether Daniels knows Howard Odum and Rupert Vance, two icons of liberal sociology. He does. "That's a great University at Chapel Hill," the man replies.

William E. Leuchtenburg is Kenan Professor of History at the University of North Carolina at Chapel Hill and the author of several books about Franklin D. Roosevelt, the New Deal, and the American Presidency.

Phillip Manning

---

on

Aldo Leopold's

A Sand County Almanac

PHILLIP
MANNING
DAVID TERRY 8/96

Many Southern boys grow up with a shotgun in one hand and a cane pole in the other, but not me. As a teenager in South Carolina in the 1950s, my interests were books, beer and girls. Then, it was college and graduate school, a life of test tubes and equations. To get away from labs and blackboards, my wife and I began taking short camping trips to the mountains. Soon, I was reading *Field & Stream* and dreaming of salmon fishing and pheasant hunting. Finally, when I went to work for Dupont as a research chemist, my first big purchases were a 12-gauge Remington shotgun and a fishing rod with a Mitchell 300 spinning reel.

A true Southerner at last!

I became hooked on the outdoor life, on early mornings in the spring surf with the backwash of waves tugging at my waders and on fall afternoons in warm, brown cornfields with the smooth stock of a 12-gauge shotgun cool against my cheek. Still, queasiness sometimes held me back as a hunter; I remember holding the warm, brown neck of a wounded dove between my thumb and forefinger and choking its life away, while its wings beat futilely against my hand. I felt like a murderer.

Then, in 1970, during a business trip to New York, I stopped in a hole-in-the-wall bookstore and paid 95 cents for a paperback titled *A Sand County Almanac* by Aldo Leopold. The book is a classic in the literature of conservation, a fact borne out by its presence in almost every bookstore in America nearly 50 years after its publication in 1949.

At the time, though, I'd never heard of Leopold; I bought the book because the cover blurb indicated that the writer was an outdoorsman. I thought maybe it was a collection of hunting and fishing stories.

That evening in my hotel room, I realized it was something else. I came upon a paragraph in the foreword that stopped me cold: "Conservation is getting nowhere," Leopold wrote, "because it is incompatible with our Abrahamic concept of land. We abuse land because we regard it as a commodity belonging to us. When we see land as a community to which we belong, we may begin to use it with love and respect."

I wasn't a religious person, but, like many outdoorsmen of that time, I did, in fact, have an Old Testament concept of land. I believed it was mine to conquer and exploit. It was "us" against "them." "Us" being mankind, "them" being all other living things. You went into the field and took what you wanted.

Leopold, I learned from the book, was a Yale-educated forester who joined the U.S. Forest Service in 1909. From then until 1933, when he began teaching at the University of Wisconsin, he witnessed the precipitous decline of our country's wildlife as loggers leveled ancient forests and industries poured waste into rivers.

But Leopold was also a hunter. In one passage, he describes a hunt he had participated in as a young man. After firing into a pack of wolves — a common practice in those days, when predators were hated and killed on sight — he walked toward a wounded female and watched the "fierce green fire dying in her eyes." "Since then," he said, "I have lived to see state after state extirpate its wolves. I have watched the face of many a newly wolfless mountain, and seen the south-facing slopes wrinkle with a maze of new deer trails. I have seen every edible bush browsed, first to anaemic desuetude, and then to death. In the end the starved bones of the hoped-for deer herd, dead of its own too-much, bleach with the bones of the dead sage, or molder under the high-lined junipers."

Extinguishing that "fierce green fire" was a turning point for Leopold, the event that sparked his metamorphosis from trigger-happy hunter to thoughtful conservationist. Reading about it changed me, too. Gradually I lost interest in hunting. I realized that I, too, would rather see that fire in the eyes of a living creature than put it out. I began to think of the land as a community of life, not just a place that provided game birds. I began to see our rivers and seas as a complex, incompletely understood, ecosystem, not just as places to catch fish or dump wastes.

The most marked-up chapter in my tattered old paperback is near the end of the book, "The Land Ethic." In it, Leopold tells how Odysseus, on returning from the wars in Troy, hanged some slave girls in his household because he suspected they had misbehaved during his absence. "The hanging," Leopold wrote, "involved no question of propriety. The girls were property. The disposal of property was then, as now, a matter of expediency, not of right and wrong." He compared Odysseus' treatment of his slaves to our own treatment of the land.

All ethics, Leopold said, "rest upon a single premise: that the individual is a member of a community of interdependent parts." He then proposed a new ethic, a land ethic, which "changes the role of *Homo sapiens* from conqueror of the land-community to plain member and citizen of it. It implies respect for his fellow-members, and also respect for the community as such."

Leopold never saw his book in print. In April 1948, after years making the rounds of publishers, *A Sand County Almanac* was accepted by Oxford University Press. A week later Leopold's heart gave out while he was helping a neighbor fight a wildfire in his beloved Wisconsin sand country. Nonetheless, his land ethic — which suggested that we conserve entire wild communities, not just game animals and pretty birds — eloquently redefined conservation, and his book became the bible for the environmental movement of the 1970s.

Since then, the conservation movement has waxed and waned. The Clean Air and Clean Water Acts, enacted in the 1970s, are under attack in Congress. The Endangered Species Act is itself endangered and may soon go the way of the passenger pigeon. "Property rights" groups are insisting that Leopold was wrong, that property owners can and should do with their land whatever they choose, regardless of the consequences to their neighbors or the land-community.

This approach to land-use is dangerous. Clear-cutting, for example, destroys the forests that supply the oxygen we breathe; destructive agricultural practices allow our topsoil to wash into the sea; and hog wastes foul our rivers, making our water undrinkable, while developers pave over the wetlands that could purify it.

Leopold understood the need to educate the public, and he employed the new science of ecology to do it. He believed that a man is less likely to destroy what he understands. "The urge to comprehend must precede the urge to reform," he said. That sentence struck a responsive chord in me when I read it in 1970, but it took me 15 years to act on it. Since then, however, I have been learning about the land and passing on what I learned by writing books and articles about natural areas.

Today, as I reread *A Sand County Almanac*, I find no false notes in it. Leopold wrote from the heart; there was nothing trendy about him. And — in an age that encourages short-term economic growth — we must relearn the lessons Leopold taught about the land as community. The air we breathe, the water we drink, and the soil that feeds us depend on it.

Phillip Manning is a naturalist whose several books include Afoot in the South: Walks in the Natural Areas of North Carolina.

Tim McLaurin

---

on

The Autobiography of Malcolm X

TIM
McLAURIN
DAVID TERRY 8/96

In 1970, I was 16 years old, full of hormones and emotions, and thoroughly confused by that troubled time.

One minute I was drawn toward the promises of peace and love made by hippies, and the next minute I was jerked backward by my working-class roots.

I believed in integration but could not drown out the voice in the back of my brain that reminded me I had ancestors who were members of the Ku Klux Klan.

One day I was browsing through the school library when I picked up a thick paperback book with a picture of a black man pointing his finger right at me. I checked out the book and started reading *The Autobiography of Malcolm X.*

And his words hit me like stiff rights to the gut.

Our school district had been integrated for three years. I played on the basketball team with blacks and had worked in the tobacco fields with them since I was eight years old, but that was about as far as true fraternity went; the lines still were clearly drawn.

Reading the book, I was suddenly confronted with a black man who did everything I was conditioned to believe he should not.

In the beginning, he dated white women, hustled and conned white men, and talked pure trash the whole time he was doing it. After his conversion to Islam, he spoke of whites as devils and the cause of every problem on Earth. Close to the end of his life, he began to speak of the brotherhood of mankind.

Twelve years later, I'd logged a lot of miles in my life. Military service, marriage and divorce, college and another marriage. I was living with my wife in Tunisia in North Africa, where we were serving as Peace Corps volunteers. I was also writing my own stories at night, huddled under a blanket over a portable typewriter.

As Malcolm X had done, I wrote about the people I knew best. I wrote about men and women who worked hard and drank hard and played hard.

Before I left the States, I'd shown a manuscript I completed to a friend in Raleigh; She was an educated, middle-class New England native. She read my story and then commented, "I like the writing, but who wants to read about a bunch of rednecks who fight and cut each other? Most people who buy books couldn't relate to them."

Her comment haunted me. It seemed every story I wrote had a drunk or a truck driver or a barroom fight in it. Fortunately, a friend handed me a book he had bought one day at the American embassy and said he thought I'd like it. I did. The book was about drunks and street people and the hard life of Albany, New York. It was titled *Ironweed*, written by some guy I'd never heard about — William Kennedy. The book went on to win the National Book Award and the Pulitzer Prize.

I carried my manuscript back home, and it was published as my first novel.

Malcolm X's story and Kennedy's tales impart strong truths about the people who made me uncomfortable.

The Autobiography of Malcolm X was a journey that often made me angry and sometimes sad; it even made me laugh occasionally. I realized I witnessed the transformation of a man who rose from ignorance and prejudice to wisdom and tolerance. The book mirrored my biases and forced me to realize that I was not the center of the universe. It also showed me that problems between races and classes of people were not limited to the South.

I am of a class of Americans who live from paycheck to paycheck and always earn that check. Kennedy's novel forced me to look beyond the appearance of a man and to try and search his soul.

Indeed, Malcolm X and Kennedy wrote of worlds vastly different from the lives of most people who buy and read books. But their stories of misfits and deadbeats and heroes showed me that my own "redneck," hard-living Southerners have stories to tell, and that their lives are important as long as I write from the heart.

Our characters exist, be it in Albany, NewYork, or New York city or Fayetteville. They are black and white women and men and children mired in ignorance and shackled by drugs, booze, bad jobs, poverty and rage. But they survive on dreams, grit and hope. I pity the plight of some, and others I view with contempt. Every now and then, one of these people appears with a story that makes me stand up and applaud.

Tim McLaurin, a Fayetteville native, has served in the Marine Corps, the Peace Corps, and toured with a carnival with his snakes. The author of several novels, including Cured by Fire *and* Woodrow's Trumpet, *he currently teaches at N.C. State University.*

Toril Moi

---

on

Simone de Beauvoir's

The Second Sex

TORIL
MOI

I never met Simone de Beauvoir. For me, as for the majority of her readers, she was not a real person, but a mythic figure. I first read *The Second Sex* in an abbreviated translation in the aftermath of 1968. I was 15 and lived in a rented room in a very small Norwegian town where I attended high school. Reveling in my newfound freedom, I immediately identified with the author. To me, she was an utterly amazing creature: a real-life example of an Independent Woman. And she had lovers as well, even a very famous and intelligent one called Jean-Paul Sartre. In my youthful imagination, sex and intelligence became inextricably linked: Never would I settle for a stupid man, I resolved.

Norwegian country villages were notoriously lacking in jobs for women, so my own experience of the lives of adult women did not offer much variety. All were housewives. The few who did not have children were said to be trying hard to have them, and were to be pitied until they succeeded. But Simone de Beauvoir proved with style, elegance and intellectual conviction that it was possible for a woman not to want any children at all: Indeed, it seemed to me then that her example conclusively showed that it was much better not to have any. At the time I never really questioned my own — and her — elitism: For the implication was, after all, that only exceptional women could hope to escape the fate of motherhood and housewifery.

More or less unconsciously, then, I used the glorious example of de Beauvoir as a model for my own struggle against my mother, setting out as best I could to become a childless, intellectual woman with a lover or two. And, of course, to go to Paris. Learning French suddenly became an obvious necessity — the idea of becoming an independent woman stuck in my puritanical mountain village somehow didn't bear contemplation. Living abroad, becoming an intellectual, not having children: In my desire to avoid becoming like my own mother, I have ended up copying that other mother, Simone de Beauvoir.

On closer inspection, however, the differences between us are just as striking. For although she traveled widely, de Beauvoir lived her whole life within the same square mile of Paris. Her grave is one block away from her birthplace. For her, exile was a punishment inflicted on writers by totalitarian regimes. She never learned to speak other languages very well. I, on the other hand, have chosen to live abroad, first in England and then in the United States. I write my books in English and not in my mother tongue. I will probably not be buried next to the 1,000-year-old church on the west coast of Norway where my grandparents and great-grandparents have been laid to rest.

When I came to write my new book, *Simone de Beauvoir: The Making of an Intellectual Woman*, the title imposed itself from the start. Clearly, the wish to understand why and how de Beauvoir became de Beauvoir also expresses my wish to understand my own trajectory from the Norwegian fjords to the forests of North Carolina. But I would never write a book that didn't reach beyond the merely private. If my thoughts and feelings about de Beauvoir are of interest to others, it is because she remains the emblematic intellectual woman of the 20th century. In my book I try to understand the hostile as well as admiring responses to de Beauvoir.

More than any other group of women, intellectual women are enjoined to choose between their minds and their bodies. In her life, her novels and in her great feminist essay *The Second Sex*, Simone de Beauvoir always refused to accept that divide. For her — and for me — an intellectual woman should never have to sacrifice her senses for her intellect. It is, after all, not as if intellectual men have ever been required to do so. And yet we still live in a culture in which women don't need to have a Ph.D. to fear that "excessive" intellectual activity will make men think of them as ugly blue-stockings or dried-up spinsters. This fear, I think, is particularly strong among young women uncertain of their sexuality and their desires, and it often interferes with their education and ambitions. The alternative, for some, is to fall madly in love with an intellectual man, in the hope that he, at least, will value the mind as well as the body.

This, at least, is what happened to de Beauvoir. At the age of 21, she met the 24-year-old Jean-Paul Sartre. One day in June 1929, about three weeks after they first met, the two students sat down in the Luxembourg Gardens in Paris to discuss philosophy together. For the first time, she tried to present her own philosophical thoughts to him, rather than just discussing the philosophers on the exam syllabus. "In the end I had to admit I was beaten," she writes in her memoirs. "'I am no longer sure what I think, nor whether I can be said to think at all,' I noted, disconcerted, in my diary." In this moment, she decided that he was the real philosopher, and that she would never be more than a philosophical disciple. My book is an attempt to understand the complex web of personal, institutional and public factors that led de Beauvoir to define herself as "second only to Sartre."

When I took a closer look at de Beauvoir's relationship to Sartre, it appeared less glamorous than I had imagined when I was 15. Rereading her memoirs and studying the recently published letters, I discovered that she regularly and throughout her life, particularly when she had too much to drink, broke down and cried violently and desperately, often in bars or cafes. People who witnessed such crises were terrified. Other studies have emphasized de Beauvoir's cool success, her indomitable will to succeed, as well as her unbreakable commitment to Sartre. I have reached rather different conclusions. It now appears to me that her brilliant achievement and worldwide successes were lined with sadness, loneliness and depression; the successful Simone de Beauvoir — the very icon of female independence — was vulnerable, fragile, sad and desperately yearning for love.

Her letters and wartime diaries revealed that by the time she was in her early 30s, de Beauvior was continuously involved in torturous and rather shabby relationships. She carried on a long, secret affair with the lover of her best friend. She had affairs with a number of young women and shared some of them with Sartre. At the same time Sartre seduced more women than he could count. Together the two of them schemed and plotted to get rid of lovers who did not accept the supremacy of the parent-couple.

Why did de Beauvoir want to live in this way? What was in it for her? In my view, the answer is that she preferred emotional turmoil and intensity of just about any kind to the horrifying feeling of emptiness that invaded her every time she felt forsaken by Sartre. In spite of her heroic effort to keep up an appearance of happiness and contentment, de Beauvoir suffered much pain from Sartre's continuous involvement with other women. By sticking loyally to him, moreover, she made it impossible for her to express her own unhappiness. Instead she tried to fill her loneliness, her emotional void, with intense affairs with others. But these others were always surrogates, never satisfying, never the real thing. In spite of her brilliant fame and worldwide success, Simone de Beauvoir waged a continuous struggle to convince herself that she was a happy woman.

When I started to understand all this, I felt no need to take de Beauvoir to task for failing to live up to the image of perfect feminist independence that I had imagined in my youth. Like the rest of us, Simone de Beauvoir was torn by the conflicts of a patriarchal society. Like the rest of us, she needed love and friendship. Like the rest of us, her desire for love sometimes made her act against her better judgment.

I am no longer a 15-year-old schoolgirl. I no longer

need idealized role models. Nor do I need to heap scorn on her to make myself feel better about my own imperfect choices. We do not need to be perfect, she teaches us, we simply need never to give up.

Toril Moi is a professor of literature and romance languages at Duke University. Her biographical study, Simone de Beauvoir: The Making of an Intellectual Woman, *was published in 1994.*

Robert Morgan

---

on

Leo Tolstoy's

War and Peace

ROBERT
MORGAN
DAVID TERRY 8/96

The fall of 1958 was the last time we grew sorghum cane and made our own molasses on our small farm in the Blue Ridge Mountains. After school, I worked long hours cutting and stripping the stalks, then feeding them into the mill while Daddy and Uncle Abe boiled the molasses syrup over the furnace. The sweet steam mixed with the sour smell of leaves in ditches and marshy places along the creek. I had been reading Dickens, and I was thinking of pickpockets and back alleys of London. I was also thinking of tramping the woods with my squirrel rifle. I was looking forward to high school, and I had a sense my world was about to change.

That same fall, the Henderson County Library began sending a bookmobile to the county's smaller communities. It was really just an old repair truck outfitted with shelves where the tool trays had been. The bookmobile arrived in the Green River Baptist Church parking lot on the first Monday of every month. When I first heard it was coming, I ran to meet it.

I had never seen so many books before. The two women in charge opened the back doors of the truck and revealed more volumes stacked inside. I went through the shelves on the left, touching faded bindings and torn dust jackets. My eyes stopped on a book in maroon cloth with *War and Peace* stamped in gold on the spine. It was the thickest tome I had ever seen, except for the Bible and the dictionary. I lifted it off the shelf and felt the weight, the substance of it. I had seen *War and Peace* advertised in the Sears & Roebuck catalogue as "the greatest novel ever written." This was the book I had been looking for.

• • •

I don't ever remember being without books. We didn't have enough money to buy a car or truck or tractor, and we had to borrow a horse, but we had a few novels and history books and copies of *National Geographic* on the mantel. Some religious tracts and pamphlets had been sent by radio preachers after Mama and Daddy had mailed them a dollar. There was also a big dictionary that my great-grandpa must have bought, along with a few other books that were in boxes in the attic, when he wagoned hams and produce down to Augusta, Georgia, in the days before the railroad reached the mountains.

The Bible was the book the grown-ups talked about most in our house. Daddy and my grandpa argued constantly about whether the prophecies had been fulfilled.

"I figure Stalin is the anti-Christ," my grandpa said.

"Hitler was the anti-Christ," Daddy said. "And I figure the Rapture will come by the end of this century."

"It says the world will end in fire," my grandpa said. "I reckon Stalin will blow it up with the A-bomb."

When my sister and I were little, Mama and Daddy read to us every night by the fireplace. They read from the Bible, and they read from a book of children's stories that included *No Penny* and *The Little Red Hen*. The year before I was to begin school, Mama bought a primer and taught me to read about Dick and Jane and Sally and their dog Spot. I was impressed that their dad left every morning for work in his Sunday suit.

When I began school, I was bored because I already knew how to read and write and count. As a result, I wasted my time daydreaming or teasing the other students. There was no library at Tuxedo Elementary School, but there was a small shelf of books at the back of each classroom in grades four and above. When I reached the fourth grade, I started checking out books and reading one each day. I read *Old Yeller* and *Farmer Boy* and all the *Little House on the Prairie* series. I read the Hardy Boys books, and found it hard to believe there were so many stories in the world.

By the time I reached the sixth grade, I discovered Jack London and the fiction of the far north. I read *White Fang* and *Call of the Wild* and *To Build a Fire*. I thought constantly of the Klondike and the Yukon and the Northwest Territories. In the novels of James Oliver Curwood, I followed the Mounties and trappers under the northern lights.

There had been a lot of talk lately about "beating the Russians." In the aftermath of the first Sputnik, we had been told by our teachers that it was our duty to study science and math to help the Free World compete with the Soviets. I took the exhortation seriously and knew that I would study engineering or physics someday if I could get a scholarship. But already, secretly, I was thinking of other ambitions. I had begun to take piano lessons, and practiced Mozart and Bach on the piano longer and longer hours. I wrote poems and stories in my school notebooks.

But once I got Tolstoy's big novel in my hands, I seemed to think of nothing else that fall. I did not have a reading lamp, so I read sitting on my bed in the light of one overhead bulb. Once I started *War and Peace*, I knew this was a different kind of novel from any I had read before. It was a story about people, and the minds of people, but also about history and the logic of history. It had to be read slowly, and it rewarded the reader sentence by sentence and paragraph by paragraph, and not just through the unfolding of the plot. It was a story of insight as well as action.

The novel had a different pace and scale. The scenes were in ballrooms and drawing rooms, and the characters included counts and princesses and army officers. But the detail was so vivid and real I felt intimate with the Imperial world spread out so slowly and thoroughly: "The young Princess Bolkonsky had come with her work in a gold-embroidered velvet bag. Her pretty little upper lip faintly darkened with down, was very short over her teeth, but was all the more charming when it was at times drawn down to meet the lower lip. As is always the case with perfectly charming women, her defect — the shortness of the lip and the half-opened mouth — seemed her peculiar, her characteristic beauty."

Each day that fall I could hardly wait to get the cows milked, and the corn shelled for the chickens, so I could run back to read about the Bolkonsky estate outside Moscow, or the party where Pierre ties a policeman on the back of a bear. Sitting in the cold bedroom with only the dim light above me, with rain tapping on the oak trees outside, I wandered over the Napoleonic battlefields with Pierre, among the confusion and carnage.

We are told that before Tolstoy and Stendhal all portraits of war had been heroic: Homer and Virgil, Milton and Tasso. But Tolstoy showed us the panic and disorientation, the helplessness of the individual in battle. The sarcastic portrait of Napoleon is a kind of comic relief, balancing the sympathy for Pierre, Prince Andrey, the young Rostov. One of the passages I have never forgotten is the vision of the deep blue sky above the battlefield that Prince Andrey sees when he is wounded.

"Above him there was nothing but sky — the lofty sky, not clear but still immeasurably lofty, with gray clouds creeping quietly over it. 'How quietly, peacefully, and triumphantly, and not like us running, shouting, and fighting, not like the Frenchman and artilleryman dragging the mop from one another with frightened and frantic faces, how differently are those clouds creeping over that lofty, limitless sky. How was it I did not see that lofty sky before?'"

The greatest writers never lose sight of eternity, it has been said, no matter how loud or twisted the events in the foreground. Tolstoy's ability to describe life in drawing rooms and country houses, city clubs and army barracks and headquarters, answered a hunger I did not know I had about how the world works, or had worked. His society women, politicians and generals, rakes and spongers, were more real to me than most of the people I knew in Green

River.

The essay chapters on history and destiny — the very passages that more mature readers often skip over — were among those that stirred me most profoundly. Even so, I was unprepared for anything as romantic as the scene where Prince Andrey hears Natasha at her window in the moonlight.

"She was evidently leaning right out of the window, for he could hear the rustle of her garments and even her breathing. All was hushed and stonily still, like the moon and its lights and shadows. Prince Andrey dared not stir for fear of betraying his unintentional presence.

"'Sonya! Sonya!' he heard the first voice again. 'Oh how can you sleep! Do look how exquisite! Oh, how exquisite! Do wake up, Sonya!' she said, almost with tears in her voice. 'Do you know such an exquisite night has never, never been before.'"

As I chopped wood or picked corn in the cool October afternoons, I was really thinking of Natasha and Sonya, of the down on the little princess's upper lip, of old Prince Bolkonsky working at his lathe and of the exhilarating foxhunt over the steppes that lasted all day.

Each afternoon and weekend that fall I hoped it would rain, so I could stay in my room and read. Sometimes I rested my eyes by practicing on the old piano. But mostly I sat cross-legged on the bed reading Tolstoy in the gray light of our house in the woods. The best part of the story was still to come.

Near the end of the novel, while Pierre is being led away as a prisoner of the French as they flee Russia, he comes to know a fellow prisoner, an old peasant named Platon Karataev. Even as they are cold and hungry and force-marched day after day, the old man never loses his liveliness and friendliness. The reader shares Pierre's wonder at the old peasant's resilience. Platon Karataev is a kind of philosopher; he encourages Pierre to see meaning in the simple details of his life, in eating and sleeping and talking, in the living of a life day after day. Pierre has spent his previous years searching for meaning and self-knowledge.

"He had sought for it in philanthropy, in freemasonry, in the dissipations of society, in wine, in heroic feats of self-sacrifice, in his romantic love for Natasha; he had sought it by the path of thought; and all his researches and all his efforts had failed him. And now without any thought of his own, he had gained that peace and that harmony with himself simply through the horror of death, through hardships, through what he had seen in Karataev. Pierre recognized the truth of the main idea. The absence of suffering, the satisfaction of needs, and following upon that, freedom in the choice of occupation, that is of one's manner of life, seemed to Pierre the highest and most certain happiness of man. Only here and now for the first time in his life Pierre fully appreciated the enjoyment of eating when he was hungry, of drinking when he was thirsty, of sleep when he was sleepy, of warmth when he was cold, of talking to a fellow creature when he wanted to talk and to hear men's voices."

This seemed like the best wisdom I had encountered at the age of 14. It still does to the 51-year-old reader today.

In the concluding sections of the book, Tolstoy shows us the married couples, Pierre and Natasha, Nicolay and Marya, long after the Napoleonic wars are over. They are raising their families, looking after their estates, worrying about the details of their households. These chapters reinforce the insight of the old peasant, that the meaning of things is in the living of our lives day after day.

Still, Pierre is not satisfied. He wants to do more. He would like to influence the reform of society. "All my idea really is that if vicious people are united and form a power, honest men must do the same. It's so simple, you see."

Reading *War and Peace* suggested to me that I did

not live just in the Green River valley, in the Blue Ridge Mountains, but in the world, in the stream of history, and that my thoughts and ambitions were much like those of people everywhere. I saw that the Blue Ridge Mountains were everywhere, and that the gift of fiction was to connect me to everybody.

Robert Morgan hails from the Blue Ridge Mountains of North Carolina. He is the author of several books of poetry and fiction, including The Truest Pleasure. *He has taught creative writing at Cornell University for 25 years.*

Howard Owen

---

on

The Chip Hilton Books

DAVID TERRY 96
HOWARD·OWEN

In the first novel I ever read, there is a hero, and he has a quest. He must overcome great odds and defeat or neutralize formidable foes. En route, he achieves a certain grace by putting others ahead of himself, by subjugating pain and disappointment, by sacrificing for the greater good. In the end, the Grail is his.

And then he, Soapy, Speed and the rest of the gang all go out for sodas and milkshakes.

Two passions dominated my tender years: sports and reading. My idea of a day well spent was a Saturday bouncing between the First Baptist Church basketball gym in Fayetteville and the public library next door.

But while I loved playing sports, it became evident to me early on that sports were not going to love me back. I would be the gangly forward who stopped growing too early, the good-field, no-hit first baseman, the pulling guard who dreamed of being a sure-handed end.

This did not keep me from devouring everything related to sports. I read baseball box scores even more avidly than I now read the stock-page agate that determines whether my golden-years' diet is caviar or cat food. If I wasn't playing ball, I was watching it on TV.

So, when my aunt and uncle gave me my first three Chip Hilton books one Christmas in the late 1950s when I was about 10, they gained instant induction into the Gift Hall of Fame.

Each book — and, through gifts and purchases, I got them all and read each one at least twice — was built around a sports season. But there was a parallel theme, a problem that tested and exhibited Chip's character. Maybe it was a new kid in town who hid his insecurity behind false bravado. Maybe it was a coach who was leading the players down the wrong path. Maybe it was the frustration of injury. The way Chip dealt with these dilemmas told a young boy much about the way honorable people act. If you lost the big game because you did the right thing, you were still a winner.

The author, Clair Bee, was a successful college basketball coach whose career ended when one of his teams at Long Island University was tainted by the point-shaving scandals of the early '50s. Perhaps the books were a catharsis, a way to remake the world the way he wished that it had been.

There were, I believe, 21 books in the Chip Hilton series (I still have 11 of them on my top bookshelf, the shelf reserved for books you want to keep but will never read again). They have titles like *Touchdown Pass*, *Pay-Off Pitch* and *Dugout Jinx*. Some of them have exclamation points at the end: *Strike Three!*, *Ten Seconds to Play!* They follow a boy from his junior year in high school through college. Chip Hilton played the real sports, the ones with which every boy in the 1950s grew up: football in the fall, basketball in the winter, baseball in the spring and summer.

This how-you-played-the-game ethos was a logical evolution from the Frank Merriwell books of the previous generation, but the Chip Hilton series seems hopelessly out of date now. The hero, in addition to being brilliant and what we used to call a natural athlete, is selfless, hard-working and pure of heart. He takes care of his widowed mother, eschews a college scholarship and works at the soda shop while helping State U. to glory. (Chip's dad, now there was a man: a former All-American who became a chemist and was crushed to death saving a careless worker's life.)

To someone closing in on 50 in the last days of a wise-guy century, Chip Hilton is a little hard to take at times, a little too good to be true. Does this feeling diminish him, or me?

Chip helps friend and foe alike, beating down the

most mean-spirited cynic with his muscular Christianity. Don't get me wrong; there is no overbearing Religious Right message in the books. Chip showed rather than told.

Bee did build a romantic interest into the series, although Chip seems almost oblivious to her. His platonic girlfriend, the lovely Mitzi Savrill, was described by Paul Woody, a compatriot at the *Richmond Times-Dispatch* and fellow Hiltonphile, as a combination of Marilyn Monroe, Madame Curie and Mother Teresa. She was the pinnacle of untouchable female perfection. You knew you were getting too old for the Chip Hilton books when you found yourself thinking, after Chip had blissfully ignored Mitzi's interest for the umpteenth time, "I wish she'd try that with me."

Chip lived in Valley Falls, the perfect Middle America town in which to grow up. It was big enough to have a main drag and various neighborhoods — poor kids lived across the river on the South Side and often were Chip's nemeses — but small enough that everyone went to the same high school. (The series was written from the late '40s to the early '60s, and in the earlier books, covering Chip's high school years, African-Americans were almost invisible, much as they were in my real-life Southern world.)

Chip's friends all had nicknames like Speed and Biggie and Soapy. His high school coach, Henry Rockwell ("The Rock"), was a mixture of Vince Lombardi and Jesus of Nazareth. Everybody went to the Sugar Bowl (where Chip worked when he wasn't making all A's and all-state in three sports) for sodas and shakes after the big game.

The Chip Hilton books were the first things I ever read after the lights were supposed to be turned off. They turned what was a sometimes pleasurable, sometimes tedious activity into a compulsion. For a boy for whom the written word had previously been represented mainly by the Old and New Testaments, the sports pages, comic books and such material as was assigned to us at Sunnyside Elementary School, it came to me as a revelation that reading could enlighten and entertain at the same time.

These were novels, complete with beginnings, middles and ends, some 200 pages long each. They showed me how a story should be told, even if this information was coming in on an undetected wavelength, stored away like repressed memory for another day. Without my knowing it, they were a bridge from Uncle Scrooge to Mark Twain, Dickens and Robert Heinlein.

The Chip Hilton books also made me think about the possibility of writing, because they were based in a world — sports — with which I was familiar.

The first fiction I ever wrote, for a seventh-grade assignment, was a sports story, about a legendary minor-league home-run hitter who never makes it in the big leagues. By the time I was 13, I knew that what I wanted to do for a living was write about sports. From writing about sports to just plain writing is a small jump.

In the beginning, there was Chip, and it was good.

Howard Owen, a Fayetteville native, has worked for newspapers for 25 years, currently offering his talents to The Richmond Times-Dispatch. *His novels include* Fat Lightning, Answers to Lucky *and* Littlejohn, *which has been translated into Japanese, French and Korean. He lives with his wife in Midlothian, Va.*

Reynolds Price

on

Gustave Flaubert's

Madame Bovary

Reynolds Price
DAVID TERRY 96

Any adult whose life is changed — really changed — by the reading of a book is likely to be unstable at least if not barking mad. Think of those adults who bend their lives for Hitler's *Mein Kampf* or for that one book of the Bible — *Revelation* — which, whatever its merits, has been the occasion for nearly two millennia of lunacy.

There are certainly big exceptions to my claim. The publications of Alcoholics Anonymous, for instance, have participated in benignly altering the lives of many millions of addicts. Occasional prisoners have changed their courses radically after hours of cell time spent with philosophical or theological books.

But for most of us, the life-bending books are those we encounter in childhood — stories of children stronger than we or children worse off, stories that throw believable light on a child's most awful puzzle (which is how to grow up and matter in the world), the stories our older loved ones tell or read to us from the sacred texts of whatever creeds our family and home are founded upon (an increasing number of American children have no such luck).

The important books of my own childhood were just such stories; and I found most of them in the public libraries of Asheboro, Warrenton and Raleigh, North Carolina. For me between the ages of, say, six and 13 they amounted to promises in black and white that a boy who was plainly as hopeless as I in the skills of childhood might yet grow into a viable adult and prove able to stand with others his age in self-respecting parity.

Among my favorites was a book called *Little People Who Became Great*; it told of the childhoods of artists, inventors and statesmen, most of whom had experienced at least as hard a time as I, if not worse. Other titles were Sidney Lanier's retelling of British legends in *The Boy's King Arthur*, a splendid book about American Indians called *Wigwam and Warpath*, and Robert Louis Stevenson's durable *Treasure Island*, where a fatherless boy solves the problems of helpless adults in the midst of lost gold and literally cutthroat pirates.

But the first adult book that made a deep mark on me was, luckily, one of the masterpieces of the world's fiction — *Madame Bovary* by Gustave Flaubert. I read it in 1948, the summer I was 15, and despite its theme, it came to me in a characteristically youthful way. For several years I'd been a member of the Book-of-the-Month Club, and in 1948 I'd recently won from the club a set of the World's 10 Greatest Novels as chosen by Somerset Maugham. Most children and too many adults treasure such lists — the three tallest men with pointed ears east of the Rockies, the strongest midget north of the Pecos, the highest or deepest or coldest whatever. They help us believe that success is simple.

But I'm a little vague now on the names of Maugham's 10 novels. I'm fairly sure they included *Tom Jones*, *Pride and Prejudice*, *The Red and the Black*, *Pere Goriot*, *Moby Dick*, *Wuthering Heights*, *War and Peace*, *The Brothers Karamazov* and *Madame Bovary*. To this day, I've failed to read a couple of those, but for some reason I settled down to *Bovary* post haste on an un-air-conditioned summer day in my family home on Byrd Street in Hayes Barton, Raleigh. I read the first two-thirds over several days, increasingly drawn into Flaubert's almost invisible but iron net of hard yet seductive detail.

I'd just spent three intermittently miserable years in a small country town, so almost at once I entered the trap that awaits Flaubert's lovely farm girl. And soon I was feeling what that girl felt as she moved to town and confronted a world she was ill-trained to meet. For the first time, a writer was forcing me to feel what a character feels — the gathering panic of Emma Bovary, hot to the melting-point with romantic delusion but miserably wed to a country doctor about as romantic as a wet Labrador.

By the time I hit the novel's last third — when Emma begins to realize that she's trapped past rescue in her own dense net of debts, lies and unrewarding adultery, I was drawn ahead toward the end of the book with a fevered compulsion I'd never known. I read the last 50 pages in a powerless unbroken trance; then I went out and walked — still more than half entranced — a hot mile up Glenwood Avenue to Hobson Gattis' Five Points Pharmacy, where I bolted down the world's best toasted pimento cheese sandwich with a fountain Coke.

Nobody I knew crossed my path — if they had, I'd have likely walked straight through them — so I was alone for the first time in my post-pubescent life with a bursting head of new steamy knowledge. I'd suddenly learned, with just my eyes and my fresh young memory, all I'd ever know about self-deceived passion and the death it entails.

I'd likewise glimpsed, as if down a black tunnel, the fiery lure of the work I knew I'd follow for the rest of my life. Somehow — anyhow — I'd write my own books to capture and shake and alter for all time the minds and lives of men and women and serious children. I started that summer, with a gruesome ghost story, and I've never looked back.

Reynolds Price is James B. Duke Professor of English at Duke University. His most recent novel is The Promise of Rest.

John Shelton Reed

on

the Agrarians'

I'll Take My Stand

JOHN SHELTON REED

The old rap on Southerners is that more of us write books than read them, and for a century or so after Appomattox it was certainly true that the South wasn't much of a literary market. But that doesn't mean that we haven't taken books seriously down here.

In fact, we may even have taken them more seriously than other Americans. Would antebellum whites have passed laws forbidding slaves to read if they thought it didn't matter? Would the Gideons (headquarters: Nashville, Tennessee) do what they do if they didn't believe in the transforming power of the Word? Don't the episodes of book-banning that periodically embarrass enlightened Southern opinion speak to a belief that reading can change people's lives? When New York Mayor Jimmy Walker remarked that no girl was ever ruined by a book he revealed his contempt for books, or possibly for girls. Anyway, most Southerners — even those who think putting up with obscenity and blasphemy is the price of freedom — know better.

I can write with some conviction about the power of books, because three or four have surely changed my life, for better or for worse. One of them is a peculiar volume called *I'll Take My Stand*, a stirring defense of the South by 12 young men, most of them associated with Vanderbilt University. That book was originally published in 1930, but I didn't encounter it until 1963, when I was an undergraduate at the Massachusetts Institute of Technology.

In those early days of the civil rights movement, Southerners in New England were constantly being called on to explain the South, challenged to defend it or (more often) simply denounced for their association with it. I got my share of this, but why did I respond? Why did I care?

The South hadn't really meant much to me when I was growing up in Tennessee. But living in Massachusetts had taught me that there were many Southern things worth defending. How to defend them, though, without defending those things that, even then, were plainly indefensible? Not easy questions, not even for a college junior who thought he knew just about everything.

I had been brooding about them one day when I came across a new Harper paperback edition of *I'll Take My Stand* at the MIT bookstore. The title sounded interesting and I recognized Robert Penn Warren's name, although I'd never heard of the other authors, or the book itself. (A nice Southern touch: Among the names I didn't recognize was John Donald Wade, who turned out to be a cousin of the Duke student I was dating and later married.) Out of curiosity, I bought the volume (books were cheaper then), took it back to my room and read it straight through.

It was a revelation. Thanks to the Dayton Monkey Trial and other events of the 1920s, these young Southerners had written at a time when the South's reputation was just about as unsavory as in the early 1960s, but they, too, believed there was another side to the story, and they had set out to tell it.

It's true that the South they were defending — an overwhelmingly rural region of small, independent farmers — didn't look much like the South I knew 30 years later. In fact, I came to learn in time, some critics said it didn't look much like the South of 1930. Never mind. These "Vanderbilt agrarians" valued many of the same aspects of the South that I had come to appreciate, after leaving it: manners, religion, tradition, community feeling.

And, unlike the most conspicuous defenders of the "Southern way of life" in 1963, they were eloquent, learned and humane.

That book demonstrated to me some things I should have known but didn't: that a Southerner doesn't have to spit on his ancestors' graves to write about the South, that you can acknowledge the South's faults but love it for its virtues, and that "conservative Southern intellectual" isn't a contradiction in terms. I was ready to sign up.

Of course, my response to this book had as much to do with where and when I read it as with what it said. Later I learned that some other Southerners my age responded quite differently to it. Young men and women who stayed in the South for their education apparently seldom felt the need to defend our region. If they read *I'll Take My Stand* at all, they were likely to be scornful of it.

Ed Yoder, for instance, has written of his youthful response: "antiquarian and nostalgic in tone, neo-feudal in its economic and social views, a bit above-it-all." Another Chapel Hill alumnus tells me that his copy is full of his outraged undergraduate marginalia, most often simply "bullshit!" Both of these men have come around to a more balanced appreciation for the book in their later years, and so have I, as a matter of fact, from the other direction.

My initial response, however, was anything but "balanced," and by the time I began to have serious second thoughts, the damage was done, the die cast. That book reinforced my determination to return to the South, and by its very ambiguity encouraged me to explore — at first idly, then later for a living — just what Southernness "is." Thirty years and a number of books of my own later, I'm still at it.

John Shelton Reed is Kenan Professor of Sociology at the University of NC at Chapel Hill. The author of many scholarly books, he recently wrote 1,001 Things Everyone Should Know About the South *with his wife, Dale.*

Louis D. Rubin Jr.

---

on

Thomas Wolfe's

Look Homeward, Angel

louis d.
rubin
DAVID TERRY 8/96

In 1943, as a singularly inept private in the wartime Army, I heard some of my fellow infantry trainees extolling the virtues of a writer named Thomas Wolfe. So a little later, upon being sent by the Army to an Italian language program at Yale University (I wasn't any good at that, either), I went over to the Sterling Memorial Library and checked out a copy of *Look Homeward, Angel.*

I returned to my room, began reading, and was promptly bowled over. No writer had ever spoken so personally of and to me: "But moments of clear vision returned to him when all the defeat and misery of his life was revealed. He saw his gangling and absurd figure, his remote and impractical brooding face, too like a dark strange flower to arouse any feeling among his companions and his kin, he thought, but discomfort, bitterness, mockery."

The awkwardness of adolescence, the frustration at being unable to make creative use of one's talents, the emotional confusion, the thwarted eagerness for new experience — here they were, articulated in language, offering the revelation, at once shocking and reassuring, that someone else had also been there: "He mailed the letter, with a sense of malevolent triumph. But the moment the iron lid of the box clanged over it, his face was contorted by shame and remorse: he lay awake, writhing as he recalled the schoolboy folly of it. She had beaten him again."

Nor was that all. Having himself experienced the emotional messiness of being young, Wolfe had gone on to write novels about it, thereby demonstrating that one's youthful identity need not always remain a chaos of unfocused, wasted energy and useless sensibility, but instead could be shaped into art. The autobiographical relationship, the awareness that the storyteller was engaged in re-creating his own personal experience, was built into the way of telling.

"He makes you want to write," the novelist Nancy Hale once remarked of Wolfe. That was it; the Wolfe novels were about being a writer, and among other things, what they promised me was that my own middle-class circumstance, my experience of growing up in a small Southern city, could as appropriately become the stuff of art as might a romantic voyage on the wine-dark deep, castles in Spain or cafes in Paris. A soda fountain in the drugstore of a Southern town on an ordinary summer afternoon could be made to glow with the same kind of poetic radiance as a stroll through the Lake Country of England!

That there were limitations to Thomas Wolfe's version of the Good, the True and the Beautiful, that the clamorous rhetorical announcement of a supposedly unique sensibility soon palls without the solidity and sturdiness of human experience to back it up, that there was considerably more both to life and to the practice of letters than the impassioned assertion of unsatisfied appetite — that kind of realization would come in due time. For the would-be writer first turned on by the Wolfe novels to learn how to do his or her own writing, a progression toward a less self-centered way of viewing life was essential.

Yet without that stunning first experience of what Herman Melville called the "shock of recognition" that occurs when a writer makes the discovery of a kindred literary sensibility, the achievement of a literary vocation would have been infinitely more difficult.

What most people fail to realize is that literature is not written out of life, but out of books. When someone first sits down to compose, say, a poem, what gets written upon the paper is likely to be derivative and crammed with cliches, since our notion of what constitutes a "poem" has been compiled from all the poems that we have previously read. The same is true of fiction and drama, or any kind of imaginative writing. We begin in the only way it is possible to begin: at secondhand.

If the desire to write is genuinely important to us, those early, derivative results are bound to make us increasingly uncomfortable. Precisely at that point, when we are sufficiently dissatisfied with our failure to express what we want to say, is when the right book by the right author can come along and show us, far more clearly than we had hitherto perceived, what it is that we are really trying to write about.

Along with that revelation of our true goal, it can encourage and invigorate us by letting us see that it can indeed be done. Thereafter, if we are willing to work hard enough for long enough, we learn to peel away some of the cliches, reflex responses, and shopworn images that are preventing us from giving our own account of what we see and know.

Just about every writer-to-be, I think, including many with far greater talent than I possess, comes upon his or her Thomas Wolfe — which is to say, happens upon an author who first shows the apprentice what is possible. William Styron, for example, has described his youthful experience with Thomas Wolfe in terms quite similar to my own. For James Joyce it was the plays of Henrik Ibsen. For T.S. Eliot it was the poetry of Shelley — though, being Eliot, he found it necessary later on not just to move on but to repudiate that early influence. Before then, Walt Whitman said that "I was simmering, simmering, simmering; Emerson brought me to a boil."

Many a young American writer has received a first invigorating charge from reading Ernest Hemingway's fiction. I have had several talented young female writing students who were propelled into literary motion upon reading Carson McCullers' *The Member of the Wedding*. For others, J.D. Salinger's *The Catcher in the Rye* used to do the job very nicely. And so on.

Yet once the young writer finds a way to articulate experience with some success and personal satisfaction, what he or she ends up writing is by no means likely to be sweepingly imitative of the chosen model. Most often the influence is absorbed into what becomes the writer's own way of saying things. It may no longer be even outwardly evident. Even so, it is there somewhere, a vantage point, a lens, a way of looking.

My own first sustained attempt at a novel, at the age of 25, was imitation Wolfe, miserably thin stuff, as I soon came painfully to realize. I was in my mid-30s before I wrote any publishable literary fiction. That happened only after I had gone on and learned to absorb myself in the work of — to cite only "autobiographical" novelists — James Joyce and Marcel Proust, writers who, unlike Thomas Wolfe, had thoroughly mastered the difference between self-expression and narcissism.

In after years, when I reread the Wolfe novels, what I came to admire most were his descriptions and evocations of places, the depictions of the rich, sensuous surfaces of everyday experience, the death scenes, the comic passages, the characterizations of family members and acquaintances.

Yet those elements of Wolfe's fiction were not what had originally captivated and enthralled me. The Wolfe who had spoken up so eloquently and reassuringly back then was the novelist who rhapsodized about proud loneliness, emotional hunger and the intense ambition to escape from the prison walls of youthful and provincial limitation.

It was that Thomas Wolfe, the author of passages and scenes and episodes, no small number of which came later to seem empty, self-hallucinating, giddily rhetorical, lacking in substance and credibility, who had first opened my eyes to what I might hope some day to accomplish with such limited literary gifts as I might possess. After all these years, I remain grateful and, on balance, a bit chagrined that I have been able to put those gifts to such slight use.

Rubin

Louis D. Rubin Jr. is Professor of English Emeritus at the University of North Carolina at Chapel Hill and Founder of Algonquin Books of Chapel Hill. He is a literary critic, historian, editor and novelist. His many works include A Writer's Companion, Thomas Wolfe: The Weather of His Youth, The Heat of the Sun *and* Surfaces of a Diamond.

James Seay

---

on

William Faulkner's

That Evening Sun Go Down

DAVID TERRY 8/96
JAMES·SEAY

Some 30 or 40 linear feet of my poetry library played a minor role in the movie *The Portrait*, which starred Gregory Peck and Lauren Bacall and was filmed in and around Raleigh.

I say feet because that is apparently how prop managers have to deal with books; that is, once they determine that your books have the right look, they ask to rent enough of them to fill a designated space.

At any rate, a few feet of my library made the final cut in one scene, and another linear inch appears in Peck's hand as he descends the stairs telling Bacall that he has found a misplaced car insurance policy tucked away in a book of Richard Wilbur's poems.

Aware myself that things get misplaced in the world, I had inventoried my books before sending them out to bear witness for literature, and as it turned out one of them did not make it back home. It was a book of Whittier's complete poems, nicely bound and the pages gilt-edged. I cannot say that I felt this loss keenly — in the way, say, I would feel the loss of a book inscribed to me by a fellow writer — because Whittier is not one of my favorite poets. Some of his poems have historical value for me, and I've always liked the sound and progressive syllable-spread of his name — John Greenleaf Whittier. But his sentimentality has kept him generally unvisited on my bookshelf.

Nonetheless I did feel the loss. I had bought the book years ago in a used book shop on the Outer Banks near Nags Head, and I can still recall how, when I first picked it up, it fell open to *Snow-Bound.* This is, of course, Whittier's most famous poem, his "winter idyll," describing in nostalgic language a typical winter storm during his boyhood in rural Massachusetts and how his family is drawn into even closer intimacy as they entertain themselves around the hearth-fire and go about their farm chores despite the "chill embargo of the snow."

Closing the book and holding it with its spine in my palm, I could see along the length of its fore edge a thin line of discoloration and wear that inadvertently marked the poem's location, that brief and definitive space to which the book's readers had turned again and again.

Pilgrims, tourists, under whatever banner, they had collectively worn a path to the same place at the altar rail.

This set me to thinking of books that I have returned to over the years and how any one of them could also be expected to fall open, as did the Whittier, to a favored passage or poem or story. Likely many of your own books would fall open to those same places — Molly Bloom's closing words in *Ulysses*, the scene in *A Farewell to Arms* where Frederic Henry thinks about the dignity of the names of villages and rivers in the face of war's abstractions, Proust's tea and madeleines, probably *Among School Children* or *The Wild Swans at Coole* or *Easter, 1916* in Yeats, just about anywhere in Whitman's *Song of Myself*, *Good Country People* or *A Good Man is Hard to Find* in Flannery O'Connor. The list goes on.

It is probable also that among these books that fall open in this manner there is that one book you would identify as the ur-book, the one where it all began for you as a reader or writer. For me it would be a collection of stories I bought in West Palm Beach, Florida, when I was a junior in high school and living in a town in the Everglades. It was *The Pocket Book of Modern Short Stories*, edited by Philip Van Doren Stern, and it still falls open to Faulkner's *That Evening Sun Go Down*.

Though this is no longer my favorite work by Faulkner, the effect it had on me when I first read it is incalculable. Part of that effect was a kind of homecoming. Faulkner took me back to my native Mississippi. We were living in Florida, owing to my father's work, and though we would move back to Mississippi after my high school graduation, Faulkner provided me a vicarious return. Moreover, I was privileged to return with a changed perspective.

The literature of nostalgia is capable only of returning us to what we know — and there are pleasurable aspects to that, as there is in *Snow-Bound.* But great literature takes us back to what we know while simultaneously altering our sense of the place. We might, for example, experience a heightened sense of what is wondrous or strange or wrong with a place.

As for what was familiar, I was taken with Faulkner's rendering of small-town Mississippi. The details he chose — the types of shade trees, the qualities of darkness and moonlight, the way a ditch or a fence will figure in the history of a place — all these had an authority I recognized. It was, after all, where I had grown up.

What further distinguished this story from what I had read was the way in which Faulkner recorded human behavior — speech, gesture, stillness, silence and so on. I think for the first time I was aware of implied motive. For that and other reasons I was transported back to my birthplace with a changed awareness.

One of those characteristics is, of course, a history of racism. To say that *That Evening Sun Go Down* is about race would be reductive, but indeed the divisions and tensions between the races provide Faulkner the dramatic ground for his story. A family I would later recognize as the Compsons in other fiction by Faulkner is responding to what the father knows to be a threat against the life of a black woman who does occasional housework for them. Because of their different ages — from parents to young children — the Compsons perceive events with different degrees of understanding.

The black woman, Nancy, is waiting for her husband to come and kill her because she has been sleeping with another man, a local banker and deacon who formerly paid her for sex but then began to renege on his promises to pay. She confronted him publicly, he hit her, and, because he was white and could do so with impunity, had her arrested. Later, when she is released, it becomes apparent that she is pregnant. The Compsons are finally either unwilling or unable to intervene to protect her from her husband.

At the time I first read this story — in the mid-'50s — I was becoming sensitive to the issue of race, so that aspect of the story found its mark easily. But what was equally important was that something about the story made me aware of a complexity that had everything and nothing to do with race. I sensed that I couldn't deal with the story in the exclusive terms of theme and conflict that I was learning in my high school literature classes.

In short, here was a story that required a different kind of engagement. For the first time a writer was calling on something in me beyond fascination with story line and action and simple categories of character and conflict.

It was the beginning of that necessary realization about any art, literary or otherwise, that continues to move us: that it is finally greater than the sum of all its technical functions and anything we could summarize about its thematic concerns.

Shortly down the road it would be poets who filled my head with language I couldn't resist and a distillation of experience that fired the lyric impulse in me as nothing else could, and I would begin writing my own poems. But before that could occur I had to open Faulkner's story again and try to understand what had been kindled in my young mind.

It is usually the promise of some such understanding that draws us back to particular stories and poems and passages in books, and if someone wanted a map to our hearts, there would be no truer one than that drawn by the measure of those places where our books fall open.

Seay

James Seay is a professor of English at the University of North Carolina at Chapel Hill and director of the Creative Writing Program. His poetry and criticism hava appeared in many publications, including The Nation, The Georgia Reveiw, Antaeus, *and* American Review.

Lee Smith

---

on

James Still's

River of Earth

LEE
SMith.
DAVID
TERRY
8/96

Although I don't usually write autobiographical fiction, my main character in a recent short story sounded suspiciously like the girl I used to be: "More than anything else in the world, I wanted to be a writer. I didn't want to learn to write, of course. I just wanted to be a writer, and I often pictured myself poised at the foggy edge of a cliff someplace in the south of France, wearing a cape, drawing furiously on a long cigarette, hollow-cheeked and haunted. I had been romantically dedicated to the grand idea of 'being a writer' ever since I could remember."

I started telling stories as soon as I could talk — true stories, and made-up stories, too. My father was fond of saying that I would climb a tree to tell a lie rather than stand on the ground to tell the truth. In fact, in the mountains of southwestern Virginia where I grew up, a lie was often called a story, and well do I remember being shaken until my teeth rattled with the stern admonition, "Don't you tell me no story, now!"

But I couldn't help it. I was already hooked on stories, and as soon as I could write, I started writing them down.

I wrote my first book on my mother's stationery when I was nine. It featured as main characters my two favorite people at that time: Adlai Stevenson and Jane Russell. The plot was that they went west together in a covered wagon, and once there they became — inexplicably — Mormons. Even at that age, I was fixed upon glamour and flight, two themes I returned to again and again as I wrote my way through high school, fueled by my voracious reading. My book choices proceeded alphabetically: the B's, for instance, included Hamilton Basso, the Brontes.... At St.

Catherine's School in Richmond, during my last two years of high school, I was gently but firmly guided toward the classics, but my own fiction remained relentlessly sensational.

At Hollins College, I wrote about stewardesses living in Hawaii, about evil twins, executives, alternative universes. I ignored my teachers' instructions to write what you know. I didn't know what they meant. I didn't know what I knew. I certainly didn't intend to write anything about Grundy, Va.

But then Louis Rubin, my teacher, had us read the stories of Eudora Welty, and a light went on in my head. I abandoned my stewardesses, setting my feet on more familiar ground, telling simpler stories about childhood. But I wasn't able, somehow, to set the stories in those mountains I came from. This never happened until I encountered James Still — all by myself, perusing the S's in the Hollins College library.

Here I found the beautiful and heartbreaking novel *River of Earth*, a kind of Appalachian *Grapes of Wrath* chronicling the Baldridge family's desperate struggle to survive when the mines close and the crops fail, familiar occurrences in Appalachian life. Theirs is a constant odyssey, always looking for something better someplace else — a better job, a better place to live, a promised land. As the mother says, "Forever moving, yon and back, setting down nowhere for good and all, searching for God knows what.... Where are we expecting to draw up to?"

At the end of the novel, I was astonished to read that the family was heading for — of all places! — "Grundy."

"I was born to dig coal," Father said. "Somewhere they's a mine working.... I been hearing of a new mine farther than the head of Kentucky River, on yon side Pound Gap. Grundy, its name is...."

I read this passage over and over. I simply could not believe that Grundy was in a novel! In print! Published! Then I finished reading *River of Earth* and burst into tears.

Never had I been so moved by a book. In fact it didn't seem like a book at all. *River of Earth* was as real to me as the chair I sat on, as the hollers I'd grown up among.

Suddenly, lots of the things of my life occurred to me for the first time as stories: my mother and my aunts sitting on the porch talking endlessly about whether one of them had colitis or not; Hardware Breeding, who married his wife, Beulah, four times; how my uncle Curt taught my daddy good liquor; how I got saved at the tent revival; John Hardin's hanging in the courthouse square; how Petey Chaney rode the flood.... I started to write these stories down.

Twenty-five years later, I'm still at it. And it's a funny thing: Though I have spent most of my working life in universities, though I live in Chapel Hill and eat pasta and drive a Toyota, the stories which present themselves to me as worth the telling are most often those somehow connected to that place and those people. The mountains which used to imprison me have become my chosen stalking ground.

This is the place where James Still lives yet, in an old log house on a little eastern Kentucky farm between Wolfpen Creek and Deadmare Branch. Still was born in Alabama in 1906; went to Lincoln Memorial University in Cumberland Gap, Tennessee, and then to Vanderbilt; and came to Knott County, Kentucky, in 1932 to "keep school" at the forks of Troublesome Creek. After six years, as he likes to tell it, he "retired" and turned to reading and writing full time. As one of his neighbors said, "He's left a good job and come over in here and sot down."

Last summer he told me he had read an average of three hours a day, every day, for over 50 years. His poetry and fiction have been widely published and praised; his *Wolfpen Notebooks* came out in 1991 from the University Press of Kentucky.

In the preface to that fine collection of sayings and notes he has made over all these years, Still says:

"Appalachia is that somewhat mythical region with

no known borders. If such an area exists in terms of geography, such a domain as has shaped the lives and endeavors of men and women from pioneer days to the present and given them an independence and an outlook and a vision such as is often attributed to them, I trust to be understood for imagining the heart of it to be in the hills of Eastern Kentucky where I have lived and feel at home and where I have exercised as much freedom and peace as the world allows."

This is an enviable life, to live in the terrain of one's heart. Most writers don't — can't — do this. Most of us are always searching, through our work and in our lives: for meaning, for love, for home. Writing is about these things. And as writers, we cannot choose our truest material. But sometimes we are lucky enough to find it.

Lee Smith is the author of 11 books including Saving Grace *and has taught creative writing for more than 20 years. She recently won the Lila Wallace-Reader's Digest Fund Award, which she shared with her husband, writer Hal Crowther, and their three children.*

Elizabeth Spencer

---

on

Willa Cather's

Death Comes for the Arch-

bishop

Elizabeth
Spencer
DAVID TERRY 8/96

Remembering my childhood means harking back to Carrollton, Mississippi, seeing myself as a skinny little girl sitting out under the shade tree in the front yard in summer, or curled up in a chair in a corner in the winter, reading. Reading what? Any and everything? I'm afraid so.

No one book, I think, can change a life already set as a reader. I became a reader from being sick a good deal as a preschooler and having a mother who read aloud very well. She also had good taste in what to read: King Arthur and Robin Hood, Greek mythology, stories from the Bible, Aesop and Grimm, Homer (simplified for young readers), Uncle Remus stories, *Treasure Island* and *Kidnapped*.

My mother never lost an attractive childlike quality of her own: No matter what age she was, she could immerse herself in her reading so long as it was good enough to engage her. She would believe it as though it were fact, respond to it, identify with its characters as though they were alive, read on and on to know what happened next.

It is true she got rather tired of Edgar Rice Burroughs during my Tarzan phase, and I lost her interest altogether when I finally reached modern literature at college. She would go back to the old ones, was what she said. However, murder mysteries intrigued her like crossword puzzles in her later years.

My own reading habit grew naturally out of this sort of head start. I look back with interest on my discoveries, the road ahead being always pointed out by good English teachers, or relatives and friends. Talking books over is one of the joys you learn along with reading them. Which one changed my life? I guess it was the first one ever read to me, though it happened so early I can't even remember what it was.

But on consideration I think it must be some book read during adolescence that makes a sort of touchstone for thinking about any number of things — good and evil, history, possibilities of life, attitudes toward people. It must be a book that points out a slightly different way of looking at things, and one that can be returned to as long as one lives and be found both rich and dependable.

The book I would choose is *Death Comes for the Archbishop* by Willa Cather.

Everyone should read Willa Cather for the first time in high school. She is accessible to a young mind. Youth was one of her big subjects, recurrent as seasons in her writing. The talented young man, the gifted young woman, curious, born to small-town life, but expanding outward, seeking larger horizons without rejecting what was there in the first place or failing to give it true value.

How was this so different, and what gives it, for me, its enduring appeal? Cather's contemporaries were Sinclair Lewis and Theodore Dreiser. Lewis, too, wrote about small towns and the appeal of other places. He wrote about them, however, harshly, with contempt. I never favored that. Dreiser's dark visions summon more power than the others can muster, and though reading him is like taking a long road to despair, Cather does seem simple-minded and even thin beside him. So what is so good about her?

For one thing, she believed in goodness. Father Jean Marie Latour, an aristocratic Frenchman and a Jesuit missionary, is her hero in this book. He is so totally accepted by her that one wonders at the author's identification with her character. It's almost a love affair. He was indeed a person out of history with the real name of Father Jean Lamy. His dedication goes unquestioned, his tireless works for the mother church were both intelligent and selfless. Cather seems touched by the sensitive, aesthetic nature of this man, appointed to the hardest of bishoprics, the dry, unexplored reaches of the Southwest in the last century. Illnesses and accidents overtake him constantly.

We first discover him lost in the desert, himself and his pack animals all but dead of thirst. He prays; an oasis soon appears; Mexicans live there who want the sacraments he can bring; everyone is saved. This opening incident sets the tone.

Yet much that is evil will go on. The government is brutal to the Indian tribes, the Indians are brutal to the early Catholics, some priests are venal and corrupt, the Yankee settlers can be heartless and murderous, a rich inheritance is almost taken from the church by conniving scoundrels. But always the writer is holding to a faith that is not so simple as it may at first seem to be. Cather believes that good can prevail. It is an American trust.

Though her book may seem a defense of the Roman church, in reality it shows respect more than anything else. Cather was not a scoffer about anything, and she had learned enough to speak with authority: She did her homework. She took the Catholic version of events as accurate. But that she never became a Catholic is an interesting point. Was she talking as much about the civilizing effect of European ways on a raw country as about the actual beliefs the priests in that one-time Spanish country both revive and introduce? Her respect also goes out to Indian beliefs: She is not ready to dismiss them lightly, either.

Re-reading *Death Comes for the Archbishop*, I came to another interesting conclusion. Latour did not need confirmation of his faith — he was trained in the seminaries of his home in the south of France and in Paris, tested by some years of mission work in Ohio before going to New Mexico, appointed bishop by the Vatican. Yet we do find a conversion here and its nature is, I think, what the book is about. At the end, Latour is no longer a Frenchman out of place in a rough new world; he is an American. There is a passage near the end that I can never read without tears: Latour has returned to France, to visit his native village, family and friends, but he feels a bit sad there and unfulfilled. On his return to the Southwest he experiences what he has come to live for, the air of the new world:

"Something soft and wild and free, something that whispered to the ear on the pillow, lightened the heart, softly, softly picked the lock, slid the bolts, and released the prisoned spirit of man into the wind, into the blue and gold, into the morning, into the morning!"

I'm back under the shade tree in the front yard when I read this book. It's quite a lot to say about any writer, this many years after.

Elizabeth Spencer is the author of a dozen works of fiction, including The Light Diamonds *and* The Night Travellers. *Her stories have appeared in* The New Yorker, Southern Review, *and* The Atlantic Magazine. *She teaches at the University of North Carolina at Chapel Hill.*

Jane Tompkins

on

Robert Pirsig's

Zen and the Art of Motorcycle Maintenance

JANE
TOMPKINS
DAVID TERRY 8/96

When I read Robert Pirsig's *Zen and the Art of Motorcycle Maintenance*, it was summer in Philadelphia. I was trying to grow grass in the tiny eight-by-10 plot behind my house, walled in on all sides. The earth I dug smelled sour, and the sweat turned to slime on my skin. But the physical effort felt good and relieved an unhappiness I could do nothing about, or even fully recognize. The grass came up near the end of June, green and fine. By the end of July it had disappeared.

The task and its outcome reflected the sense of sterility I felt every day in my windowless carrel in Temple University's library. I was laboring over an essay on Richard Wright's *Black Boy*, an excruciating memoir of growing up black in the South. Though I couldn't let myself know it at the time, the author's pain and frustration harmonized with something in me.

I couldn't have been completely out of touch with myself, however, because somehow I'd had the sense to buy a hardback copy of Pirsig's novel. I'll never forget how it felt to fall under his spell. On page one I was flying with him down America's secondary roads, convinced that I was about to encounter, perhaps for the first time, something absolutely real. It was the combination of metaphysics and breakfast in roadside diners that did it — Plato and wind in your hair.

Pirsig satisfied the two great American hungers: for freedom and for reality. I felt he was the true successor to Thoreau, whose *Walden* he carried in his pack. And his voice possessed a colloquial familiarity that drew me close and assured me everything would be all right in the end. There was Zen, you see, and there was motorcycle maintenance, redemption spiritual and physical. Two for the price of one.

By the following summer my article on Wright had been turned down a couple of times. I was planning to get married but not feeling too sure about it. I'd made friends with a philosophy professor (not my intended) who rode a motorcycle and gave me rides on it, hoping that I would give him another kind of ride, which I never did. Come spring, I read *Zen and the Art of Motorcycle Maintenance* again and saw my solution. I would learn to ride a motorcycle. I would even learn to maintain one. I would blend the classic and the romantic in my life, the practical and the poetic parts of myself, as Pirsig aspired to do. Above all, I would ride into the future with all the excitement that I knew in my heart of hearts my impending union could never afford. I would be safe and in peril at the same time.

The motorcycle-riding lessons were more than I had bargained for. After each one I lay in bed at night stiff with fright. But I persisted, got my certificate, and with money I had saved bought a beautiful silver Honda CB 200, a street bike, just my size. Its chrome gleamed, its engine purred, and after the initial fear abated somewhat, riding that bike was the sexiest thing I'd ever done.

When I rode the bike, I always felt a little scared, but at the same time brave and connected to some power in the universe. That power was in the feel under me of the leather seat when my hand turned the accelerator and I and the bike moved forward as one.

Once, on my way home from school, I was mugged by a bunch of kids playing at an open fire hydrant. They drenched me with water, then tore off my watch and pocketbook. I was terrified, but I didn't care what they took so long as they didn't pull me off the bike. Somehow I managed to remain upright, I held on hard, gunned the motor, and got away. I can still feel how my body trembled in the aftermath.

The motorcycle brought out the adventurer in me

all right, but the classical side, never my forte, remained untapped. Unlike Pirsig's motorcycle, mine never broke down, so I never needed to cultivate the mechanical skills, methodical reasoning and patient faith that motorcycle maintenance was supposed to foster. But never mind. The motorcycle had given me a focus and a sense of identity in a time of confusion.

In a few years, I left the man I married when I bought the motorcycle, left him precipitately for another man, whom I subsequently married. And then I didn't need the motorcycle any more.

Many years have passed since then. The bike still sits in my garage, draped in a sheet, a ghost from the past, unvisited, and Pirsig's novel sits on a shelf upstairs, untouched. The novel, though, unlike the motorcycle, may be only biding its time. Circumstances change. Who knows what might happen if I were to read it again?

Jane Tompkins is a professor of English at Duke University and the author of a memoir, A Life in School: What the Teacher Learned, *among other books.*

Tom Wicker

---

on

The Saturday Evening Post

DAVID TERRY 8/96
TOM WICKER

In my memory of a North Carolina boyhood, it's always summer. The sky is pale with heat, the grass under my bare feet barbed with sand spurs; a watermelon is cooling in a tub of water in the back yard. My parents will not allow me to swim at Boyd's Lake because of the annual polio scare, and I spend those endless summers sitting in an old cane rocker under a green-and-white striped awning on the front porch of our house in Hamlet, a railroad town in Richmond County. I am listening to train whistles blowing, I'm reading, and I'm waiting for Durward Brown.

Durward was our mailman, in a day when mail was not only fast but certain; you could order from Sears Roebuck in Charlotte one day and get your baseball glove or bicycle parts the next, or at the latest on the third day. Durward's mail route took him past 414 Hamlet Ave. at 10 a.m., Monday through Saturday; I had no watch to set by his coming, but he was as regular as Shorty Nolan, who delivered milk in pint bottles to our front porch every morning before breakfast.

Not much of the mail Durward brought was for me, other than church brochures I seldom read. But on Monday mornings, as surely as the sun rose in the east, Durward Brown would bring my father's copy of *The Saturday Evening Post*, often with a Norman Rockwell painting on the cover.

From earliest school days, I had been an avid reader; perhaps the most valuable gift I received from my parents was their encouragement of this uncommon habit. I was not deft with my hands or with tools, as my father was; I was never the athlete that some of my friends were; I was a pushover in a fight; so I was a bookworm in a time and place when bookworms were considered weird. But not by my parents.

They believed powerfully in something abstract called "education," and they wanted me to read. Hamlet boasted no bookstore, but my parents were always willing for me to go to the library. If I spent the afternoon there (often studying *Life* magazine or *National Geographic* for photos of unclad women) or brought home an armload of books, they welcomed it as much as if I had hit a home run in American Legion Junior Baseball. Nor did they ever tell me "That's too old for you" or "You wouldn't understand that" — words that in later years I never inflicted on my children, either.

I wish I could say, therefore, that I was a serious reader. I wasn't. I feasted on Richard Halliburton. I read each and every one of the Tom Swift series. I solved every mystery confronted by the Hardy Boys and suffered with the Bobbsey Twins. My favorite reading may have been the *Baseball Joe* books. In our garage, I stashed great piles of the pulp magazines I had devoured — westerns, detective stories, *Flying Aces* of World War One.

In school, I detested *Julius Caesar* and *The Mill on the Floss*, which teachers insisted were "great" and "classic." They weren't as much fun as Captain Marvel comics or *The Boy's King Arthur* or one of my favorites, *The Scottish Chiefs*. As I grew a little older, I developed a fondness for the library's plentiful supply of romantic historical novels. I could not get through *The Last of the Mohicans*, and still can't. The most "serious" book I remember reading as a teenager was *Gone With the Wind*, which filled me with pride in my Southern heritage.

When I recall what I read as a youth, however, I think first of *The Saturday Evening Post*. On Mondays, I would run out to the sidewalk to take it out of Durward Brown's hands. I particularly loved its occasional stories about a couple of fishing boatmen, Crunch and Des, who could have been played by Humphrey Bogart and Walter

Brennan. Almost every issue would contain an installment of a mystery — often by Mary Roberts Rinehart, including one set in Charleston, South Carolina, where I had visited.

I remember, too, some hilarious yarns about Alexander Botts, a salesman for Earthworm Tractors. Sometimes one of the Tugboat Annie stories would turn up, although I believe they mostly appeared in the old *Collier's*.

There was serious reading in the *Post*, too — but I'm sorry to report that if one of the issues I eagerly perused contained, say, Faulkner's *The Bear*, or perhaps one of Scott Fitzgerald's short stories, I quickly passed it by, never having heard of either. I was, however, deeply impressed by the remarkable serials on "true crime" by John Bartlow Martin — a great journalist whose work first led me toward that field.

It's not so much the content of the *Post* that I remember. It's that after I outgrew the Hardy Boys and Baseball Joe, *The Saturday Evening Post* satisfied my hunger for reading. The *Post* not only confirmed my habit, it whetted my appetite to be a writer.

I had tasted success in high school writing the required essays and "book reports"; I became editor of our mimeographed school newspaper, the *Sandspur*; I disdained the *Reader's Digest*, with its predigested articles, though our English teacher foisted it on her students; and I came to want nothing so much as to write a story that *The Saturday Evening Post* would publish (and pay me, of course, what I later learned the magazine paid James Street, a real North Carolina writer: $5,000 for 5,000 words).

I never achieved that goal but, years later, I did publish a nonfiction piece in the *Post* (for which I was paid considerably less than $5,000). Still later, I shed real tears when the old magazine ceased publication — an early victim, I suppose, but not the last, of the corrosive national habit of watching television.

Not until I was in my 20s and a working journalist in Winston-Salem, did I take up "serious" reading. An erudite colleague, Bob Barnard — later the editorial-page editor of the Louisville *Courier-Journal* — deplored my low reading tastes and planted on me his Williams College copy of *Ulysses*, complete with classroom marginalia. I read it as a courtesy but saw immediately that I had been missing something — a lot. I set off for the public library and brought home both *The Portrait of An Artist as a Young Man* and *Dubliners*.

It was not just Joyce that I had been missing; the list goes on and on, and I will never get to the end of it, try as I might. Forty years later, I read very little current fiction — some of it is splendid, but I have so much catching-up to do. (After devouring George Eliot's great *Middlemarch* some years ago, I even re-read *The Mill on the Floss* and wished my old teacher were still alive so I could write to say how wrong I was.)

I don't think I was that wrong, however, in absorbing *The Saturday Evening Post* so hungrily. No doubt there were better things I should have been reading in those years, but I didn't know about them. It was the *Post* that nurtured me, encouraged me and I believe taught me, at a time when literacy — not necessarily literature — was more important to me than I realized. What Durward Brown never failed to bring on those long-ago Monday mornings, what I pored over with such avidity as I sat in that cane rocker beneath the striped awning, was an intoxicating taste of the only life I ever wanted to lead.

Tom Wicker is a former national correspondent and columnist for The New York Times. *The author of many works of fiction and non-fiction, his most recent book is* Tragic Failure: Racial Integration in America.